Explorations in Fatherland

This book explores the role of fathers from a broadly psychoanalytic lens, looking at fatherhood from the evolving perspective of fathers, the rest of the family, and society as a whole.

Edwards draws on her rich clinical experience spanning over 30 years to look at the issues and problems around the role of the father in clinical work with a range of patients, spanning from classical psychoanalytic thinking to fiction, myth, and iconography. These multifaceted approaches allow us to explore the complexities of fatherhood for each unit of the family and to tease out both the problems and positives associated with fathers and fatherhood. Enriched with clinical vignettes, this book shares a new outlook on how patterns of manhood or personhood evolve over time and encourages the reader not to limit paternal function to sexual or cultural binaries.

At a time when the role of men in society is ever more under debate, *Explorations in Fatherland* offers a fascinating and multi-faceted exploration of a key role for men and offers guidance to clinicians, and anyone interested in exploring the notion of fatherhood.

Judith Edwards is a retired consultant, psychoanalytic child and adolescent psychotherapist, and internationally published author, who worked for 35 years at the Tavistock Clinic. Her latest book, *Grandmotherland*, was published in 2024. She is interested in making psychoanalytic ideas more accessible to wider audiences, as she said in *Psychoanalysis and Other Matters* (Routledge): other matters matter.

'Having already treated us to a truly original and highly engaging study about grandmotherhood, Dr. Judith Edwards has now provided us with a remarkably rich and comprehensive examination of the psychology of fatherhood. Drawing upon centuries of insights from poets, novelists, musicians, historians, scientists, and psychoanalysts, and brimming with many of her own memorable clinical insights, Edwards has crafted a creative exploration, which will be of deep relevance not only to every male who has, or will, become a father but, also, to every human being who might well be the child of a father.'

Professor Brett Kahr, *senior fellow at the Tavistock Institute of Medical Psychology in London and honorary director of research at the Freud Museum London, as well as visiting professor of psychoanalysis and mental health at Regent's University London*

'Judith Edwards has a gift for revealing the meaning in everyday events. She also has a gift for making links between clinical work and the insights of novelists, poets, scientists and others. This book on fathers, bringing together testimony from so many different sources, will be of interest to clinicians, but also to anyone concerned with what it means to be human. A worthy successor to *Grandmotherland*.'

Maria Rhode, *professor emeritus of child psychotherapy, Tavistock Clinic, and child analyst, British Psychoanalytical Society*

'Judith Edwards writes "Once you start talking you don't know what you'll say", and this is the result. You will not find any other book on fathers like this; a marvellous essay by an experienced and original psychoanalytical psychotherapist who wants to "set people's mind wandering." It contains poignant personal stories of their fathers from many contributors, plus Edwards' associations from literature, poetry, science, history, art, feminist philosophy, politics, film, music, broadcasting, and psychoanalysis. Dr Edwards has succeeded brilliantly in her "invitation to colleagues to carve out their own pathways".'

Sebastian Kraemer, *honorary consultant, Tavistock and Portman NHS Trust*

In truth, what are these things I scribble, other than grotesques, and monstrous bodies, made of dissenting parts, without any certain figure, or any other than accidental order, coherence or proportion?

(Montaigne, 1700)

Explorations in Fatherland
Psychotherapeutic Reflections on Fathers and Fatherhood

Judith Edwards

LONDON AND NEW YORK

Designed cover image: © Getty Images

First published 2026
by Routledge
4 Park Square, Milton Park, Abingdon, Oxon OX14 4RN

and by Routledge
605 Third Avenue, New York, NY 10158

Routledge is an imprint of the Taylor & Francis Group, an informa business

© 2026 Dr. Judith Edwards

The right of Judith Edwards to be identified as author of this work has been asserted in accordance with sections 77 and 78 of the Copyright, Designs and Patents Act 1988.

All rights reserved. No part of this book may be reprinted or reproduced or utilised in any form or by any electronic, mechanical, or other means, now known or hereafter invented, including photocopying and recording, or in any information storage or retrieval system, without permission in writing from the publishers.

Trademark notice: Product or corporate names may be trademarks or registered trademarks, and are used only for identification and explanation without intent to infringe.

British Library Cataloguing-in-Publication Data
A catalogue record for this book is available from the British Library

ISBN: 9781032862132 (hbk)
ISBN: 9781032859569 (pbk)
ISBN: 9781003521846 (ebk)

DOI: 10.4324/9781003521846

Typeset in Optima
by KnowledgeWorks Global Ltd.

To Lorraine, with love.

Contents

About the Author xiii
Acknowledgements xiv

Introduction 1

1 The Idea and Fantasy of the Father Seen Through History 12

2 Having a Father and Being a Father 17

3 Fathers and Sons 33

4 Fathers and Daughters 45

5 Do Siblings Remember Fathers Differently? 65

6 Handing on in Identification, and Letting Go…Chh-Ch-Ch-Changes… 72

7 Having 'No Father': The Absent Father and the Single Parent 77

8 Fatherland: The Elephant in the Room 102

9 Being the Father to Our Own Stories: Seeing and Being Seen 105

10 The Stepfather 119

11	Rivalry with Fathers	121
12	Fathers in Poetry	124
	Conclusion	127
	Index	*130*

About the Author

Judith Edwards, PhD, MACP, TSP, is a retired consultant child and adolescent psychotherapist, who worked for over 30 years with fathers, mothers and their families at the Tavistock Clinic and elsewhere. She edited the collection, *Being Alive: Building on the Work of Anne Alvarez* (Routledge, 2001). A past editor of *The Journal of Child Psychotherapy,* she is internationally published, and her book of selected papers *Love the Wild Swan* was published by Routledge (2017) in their World Mental Health series. Recently she had a chapter in *Media and the Inner World* (Eds. Bainbridge and Yates, Palgrave Macmillan). Her memoir, *Pieces of Molly: An Ordinary Life* was published by Karnac (2014). 'I couldn't put it down',' said poet, writer and psychoanalyst Valerie Sinason. Her book *Psychoanalysis and Other Matters* was published by Routledge (2020) and *Grandmotherland* (Karnac/Phoenix 2024) as well as a children's book with artist Anna Park, *The Story of Solomon Swift, in which Solomon slows down, and becomes an observer of his own flight, and of life.* In 2010, she was awarded the Jan Lee Memorial Prize for the best paper linking psychoanalysis and the arts ('Teaching and Learning about Psychoanalysis: Film as a Teaching Tool: Morvern Callar', *British Journal of Psychotherapy*). In 2011 she became a Teaching Fellow of the Higher Education Academy. Apart from her clinical experience over the years, one of her principal interests has been in the links between psychoanalysis, culture and the arts, as well as making psychoanalytic ideas accessible to a wide audience. To that end she has published a pamphlet *HELP!* for parents and children about psychoanalytic psychotherapy.

Acknowledgements

Thank you so much to all to my contributors, mostly anonymous, who have helped me put together my thoughts about fathers. I am grateful to Kate Hawes, my editor at Routledge, and her team, and as always so many thanks to my friends and my family, chiefly my husband, Andrew Baldwin.

Introduction

There is, as Andrew Briggs (2023) said, sparse psychoanalytic literature, as well as limited commentary, on the role of the father. He makes the important point that the role of the biological father is vital and cannot be overlooked. And as Stendhal so famously said, a book is 'a mirror walking down a road'. What will you see in your reflection? An article called 'The Role of Father in Psychoanalytic Theory' (Jones, 2008) presents psychoanalytic ideas about the father's role in child development, organised into six different categories: (1) the father as an attachment figure, (2) the internalised 'good' and 'bad' father, (3) the father of the first separation-individuation period, (4) the father as self-object, (5) Freudian notions of the pre-Oedipal and Oedipal father, and (6) the father of the second separation-individuation period. An integrated framework is presented in an attempt to synthesise the varied and complex functions attributed to the father, followed by some reconsiderations of the father's role within the context of (1) recent father-child research, and (2) current economic and familial patterns. So read on.[1]

I hope my readers will grapple with ideas that extend far beyond the psychoanalytic realm. As I said in *Psychoanalysis and Other Matters* (Edwards, 2019), other matters matter. Let us keep the questions rolling. Whether or not you are now a father, you had one yourself to begin with, even if you were brought up by a 'single parent'. Even if present just as 'the third point', the father is truly never absent. The politics of fatherhood involves transition. Perhaps we don't sufficiently realise the psychological and indeed physiological significance of this transition – as we do for mothers (explored in Chapter 4 on fathers and daughters) – affecting the brain and cognition, the endocrine system, immunity, the psyche, the micro biome and even the very sense of self. What monumental shifts.

A Father Is Born

A father is born. But as Italo Calvino (1979, p. 24) said, 'How do we establish the exact moment in which a story begins? Everything has already begun before. The first line of the first page refers to something that has already happened.' I hope this gnomic comment will be unpacked in this book. It is vital to note that where I use the word 'fathers', partners (male or female partners: he, she or they), co-parents, cisgender or transgender may be used, so we might see the paternal function as being offered by others, regardless of sexual or cultural choices. In a political climate where disagreement may be regarded as bigotry, the influence of LGBTQ is often based on fear. Let us proceed without fear of reprisals to obtain wider points of view. It's an eclectic mix: there is something for everybody, and I hope that this will provide something more nuanced and flexible. 'Everyperson', including those who are not well versed in psychoanalytic terminology, please do not be put off.

The 'others' are, as Carlo Rovelli (2018) suggested, 'inextricably bound together' – a connection that those working with families will often explore. The symbol of white light comes to mind. In reality, when split up, white light is a rainbow of seven colours. Although there are a few more than seven chapters in this book, this shows how memories of fathers mix and meld. Erno Rubik, the Hungarian inventor of the Rubik's cube, says he is 'still learning': he was trying to solve the structural problem of moving the parts without the entire mechanism falling apart. He said he was really interested in 'the nature of people, the relationships between people and the centre', and as we twist and turn the cube, we discover that there are over 43 quintillion combinations that can be made – a little less than the square of the Earth's population. This is yet another metaphor for how we can try to line up different views of fathers to find something that feels good enough for each of us, perhaps gaining new perspectives on our pasts in the process.

Same-Sex Parents

There are many examples of such families in the social media sphere, chief among them being Elton John. Rock & Roll Hall of Fame personality Elton John keeps a busy recording and touring schedule, in no small part thanks to the support of his husband, David Furnish. The couple connected instantly in 1993 and have been together ever since. They now have two children, Zachary and Elijah, both born via surrogacy to the same mother. As was said at the time, 'The baby son of Elton John and his partner David Furnish will refer to his parents as "Daddy" and "Papa", respectively.' The words 'Daddy' and 'Papa' certainly seem somewhat less confusing than 'Mom', the choice of lesbian couple Nic and Jules in the film *The Kids Are All Right* – they are both 'Mom' to their kids.

What kids call gay parents is a relatively new question, but an important one. Although lesbians are far more likely to have children from previous (heterosexual) relationships as well as together (using a sperm donor), gay dads are still relatively rare. Barrie Drewitt-Barlow, one of Britain's most famous gay dads, who with his partner Tony had five children ranging in age from one to 11, was asked how they approached the issue. Barrie and Tony were catapulted into the limelight back in 1999, after becoming the first gay couple to have children via a surrogate. The couple made their money from a trans-Atlantic surrogacy business and a global medical research company. They split in 2019 but still live together and have remained great friends. This is so fortunate for their children: it is the acrimonious feelings after divorce that make for emotionally abused children. Another gay couple I speak to say they go by 'Mommy and Mommy2'. I wonder if this seems a bit hierarchical to Mommy2? It reminds me of when I became a teacher to 'the bottom class' at the Tavistock's Day Unit. I swiftly changed this name to 'Green Class'.

We are of course still thinking about the necessity of three: a child and two parents. At the beginning of July 2023, the Archbishop of York flagged up the notion that the start of the Lord's Prayer may be problematic for those whose experience of earthly fathers has been destructive. As he said, 'Perhaps we have laboured rather too much from an oppressively patriarchal grip on life.' Rev. Christina Rees, a campaigner for women bishops said that the archbishop had 'put his finger on an issue that has been alive for many years'. (The *Guardian*, 2023a) My then 4-year-old son declared that he and his friends had decided that 'God is a she-he'. Where does this place the third 'member' of this particular religious triune, in this particular religious wrapping paper, the Holy Ghost? There are, as I discovered, triunes embedded in every religion, whatever the wrapping paper.

In February 2023, the Church of England had already said that it would indeed consider whether to stop referring to God as 'he', after priests asked to be allowed to use gender-neutral terms: 'Christians have recognised since ancient times that God is neither male nor female.' The *Guardian*, 2023b This book starts with a question and will delve into a range of topics, including fathers (of either gender) as the third point. We may lose our preconceptions, but we will find a new way of looking at our world. Loss, yes indeed, but finding new ideas, too. We may sit on the cusp of objective re-telling and personal reflection, bearing witness to our own 'truths', as we travel towards the narratives at the heart of so many – if not all – lives, shaping so much of our human experience. The principal issue here is not 'the facts': we select memories to fit our narrative, the one to which we are committed. We tend to negate those that contradict it. More anon.

Gaze

How can we begin? In order to proceed, perhaps we need to think about the quality of our gaze:

> Somewhere in the great unsteady archive where our souls will be held, there is a special section that records the quality of our gaze. When a look or a glance intensified, when watchfulness opened out or narrowed in, due to curiosity or desire, or suspicion or fear. Maybe that is what we remember most of each other – the face of the other glancing up, the second when we are held in someone's gaze.
> (Tóibín, 2018, quoted in Wills, 2018, p. 38)

And see Chapter 1 where a busy general practitioner records his minute observations of a baby, trying to catch and keep his father's gaze … as Brecht himself declared:

> You, actor, must master the art of observation before all other arts.
> For what matters is not how you look but *what you have seen and can show us*.
> What's worth knowing is what you know.
> People will observe you to see how well you have observed.
> (Brecht, 2018, quoted in Hofmann (2018), p. 47; emphasis added)

As the Reverend Ames said to Lila in Marilynne Robinson's (2014) novel of the same name, 'Once you start talking, you don't know what you'll say.' We always have Father Time and Mother Earth managing our time together. And can poetry be our containing structure? So, we are thinking of gaze, the art of observation: what you might term grounded theory. What's that? Read on.

Grounded Theory

As Charmaz said, 'When you theorise, you reach *down* to fundamentals, *up* to abstractions, and probe *into* experience. The content of theorising cuts to the core of studied life and poses new questions about it' (2006, p. 135). Theorising means stopping, pondering, thinking again – stopping the flow of studied experience, taking it apart – looking at the life you're studying from multiple vantage points, making comparisons, following leads and building on ideas. You may not be able to foresee where you are going – *there is no marked road* – theorizing involves seeing possibilities, establishing connections and asking questions (keeping them in good repair, as Bion said). You need theoretical playfulness and an openness to the unexpected: seeing the new in the mundane same-old same-old – gerunds help us get active, i.e., 'setting up', 'getting started'. This really does prompt thinking regarding actions, large and. small. Then you can see sequences and make connections. Studying a process helps our efforts to construct theory and keep analytic momentum. Any field contains fundamental concerns and contested ideas, whether or not they have yet been theorised. Many people may disagree.

Writers must address the 'So what?' question: Why does your particular theory make a significant contribution? You need to find your argument and make it original and meaningful. It may differ now from what you set out to do and that's okay. An initial purpose brings you into a study but seldom suffices for an argument for the finished book. You build argument into each section, point by point (as I hope to do), step by step. You work at your argument; it will emerge, and it develops as thinking progresses. An argument is a product of grappling with the material, and you create it from points embedded in the analysis, as with the role of fathers in the family, whether biological and/or fulfilling the paternal role. Both parents matter, and families need fathers, as children know. We were all first created when one sperm in a million won the race and fertilised the egg. Bingo! Children need to be helped to keep positive pictures and relationships in their minds, especially after separation or divorce. As 'Families Need Fathers', the UK's leading Shared Parenting charity, declares, working collaboratively, they aim to support the end of what they call the 'hidden injustice' of parental alienation. What I hope for this book is that it will use psychoanalytic ideas but without overburdening the reader, and without the huge parade of academic references that are often such an off-putting issue for potential readers. Psychoanalysis matters, but other matters matter, too.

New Fathers

New fathers may feel a mixture of excitement and fear, as they try to find a new role in life. Are you ready? Will you make mistakes? It's a huge step: perhaps the biggest life-changing moment, apart from physical challenges that may also crop up. As is, it goes without saying of course, becoming a mother. Bonds with one's children can be as strong as iron if we work at it and 'put the time in' – even if we don't live with them full time, or if we don't share their genes. How do you get to know your baby? Perhaps underneath all the questions we may share common ground. As Ricky Emanuel (2001) said:

> The most striking thing about infant observation is that the father is by and large a missing person except in the beginning of the observation and on occasional visits. There are a few exceptions, when for example the father becomes the main caregiver in the family or is present for other reasons over a length of time. More usually, we have to intuit the role of the father in the family from observations of the baby or by the way the mother may talk about him. It is significant that the father is such a missing person in the observed family, as it reflects one of the main problems and difficulties in becoming a father, that is finding a role for himself in the new family constellation.

This book emphasises the need for a triangular structure in the mind, which enables the child (and any individual) to look at 'reality', internal and thus external, from the third point. It is interesting to note how much triangles feature in religious cultures throughout the world, including Buddhism and Islam, where it symbolises wholeness, and the Christian meme of Father, Son and Holy Ghost will be familiar to many Christian readers. In Buddhism, the Diamond Triangle consists of Ratnagiri, Udaygiri and Lalitgiri: this Buddhist complex of stupas and monasteries is situated in the foothills of north-eastern India and is the oldest recorded Buddhist site, housing relics of the Buddha himself. If astrology floats your boat, the triune is a fortunate combination. The triangle is a strong unit, symbolising fire, the strongest form architecturally, and, in Arabic, the corresponding word means love. But whatever the particular religious wrapping paper, there are some universal themes that remain relevant throughout the world.

So, if we move to the more abstract geometrical world of structures and shapes, and particularly that of the triangle, this may start to make sense. In a book about the intricate interweaving of Islamic patterns, Critchlow (1976, p. 17) describes the triangle as the first polygon: 'the minimal expression of an area, also symbolic of the minimal needs of consciousness; the knower, the known and the act of knowing'. He links this with what he calls the minimal description of our biological needs: ingestion, absorption and excretion (on a psychic level, these three functions also exist and underpin our considerations about psychic health). He talks of patterns being, like numbers, one of the fundamental conditions of existence, and, as such, a vehicle for archetypes and philosophical thought. As he says, 'What we take to be simple and "in the nature of things" has become profound to the point of our becoming oblivious to it.' Think about the triangle for a moment, oblivious as we may be to its profundity: it provides the third point, and thus a space opens up, for the child to reflect on the parental couple, see herself or himself as part of the web, but not the central point.

In psychoanalytic literature, the triangle has been a fundamental structure that originated with Freud's formulation of the Oedipal constellation of mother, father and child. The third point is seen as essential for there to develop a space for thinking (Critchlow's 'minimal expression of an area') and for separation and growth to take place. At the beginning of the infant's life, the mother-baby couple are protected by the father. Gradually, the father comes to take a more active role and presence (subsequent foetal research has suggested that the father may indeed through his voice be an active pre-birth presence for the baby developing inside the womb). The baby is then faced with what Kraemer (1988) in his article, 'The civilisation of fathers', called 'the facts of life as they are, rather than as the child believes or wishes them to be'. The paediatrician and analyst D. W. Winnicott talked of the 'progressive disillusionment' that needs to take place as the child has to relinquish the idea of being in sole possession of the mother, and comes to accept the reality of the third, the other, and to be able from his own point on the triangle to perceive his parents as a couple. As the late Paul Barrows (1995) indicated in his article, 'Oedipal issues at 4 and 44', this acceptance involves the linked concepts of knowing and being known (which again relates back to Critchlow's formulation). He suggests that the way in which the Oedipal situation is negotiated is fundamentally determined by the internal orientation of the patient towards the issue of knowledge: in particular, knowledge of the existence of the parental couple. Material is brought from two female patients, one aged 4 and the other aged 44, to illustrate this point, and the parallels that exist despite the difference of age and the consequent different form that the material takes. He also illustrates the particular use made of the defences of omniscience and disavowal in both cases, and the changes that took place in this regard through the therapeutic process.

Quoting Temperley, Barrows noted that Kleinian and post-Kleinian analysts place a different emphasis from Freud on the nature of the Oedipus complex: 'what the child has to accept is not primarily the prohibition of his incestuous wishes but the reality of the position in relation to his parents' sexual relationship'. The Oedipal situation, what Hanna Segal (1989) called 'the core complex', lies deep within the mind of any individual and continues to have vital relevance in the lives of modern families. In terms of psychoanalysis, it was Freud who discovered through his own self-analysis that the disliked third point was a vital factor in terms of subsequent development, even though the baby self may wish to 'marry' mother and annihilate the third point. A central question seems to be: Without a third to grapple with, how do we become a little Oedipus, wanting to claim mother and reject father, rather than a little Narcissus? In simpler words, how do we see ourselves as having been produced by the parental couple, rather than seeing ourselves as springing fully formed from nowhere, entranced by our own image (as Narcissus gazed at himself in the pool), or forever attached only to our mothers?

If the reader feels confused, then that, as Bion opined, is the way towards further creative thinking. The psychoanalyst Wilfred Bion resisted being a 'messianic' figure, a revered guru with a hotline to God, whomever she or he may be, and valued the process of thinking together, as we keep our questions in good repair. The solace of a language of certainty can preclude having a wider view, and in the face of the anxiety that this wider view may produce, there is a tendency to collapse into a split paranoid-schizoid state. What do we dare to believe or disbelieve? These questions remain vital as we engage in the process of talking and thinking together, externally and also internally: a kind of parliament. Culture, politics and economics shape our reactions. Can this even be fun? This may be the nearest to 'the whole truth' that we can get. Disguised clinical material, from myself and others, as I indicated above, is included. As Ricky Emanuel (2001) said, 'Purely psychoanalytical theory, by itself, is not sufficient to understand many of the complex mixed states carried by many children seen by child psychotherapists.' (*These are the children who come from 'single-parent' families or suffer from bereavement and loss of the absent father – a complex mixture of forces, internal but also external – JE*)[2] Mixed forms of understanding are needed. Psychoanalytic thinking and 'hard' science are not the same but need to be brought into active dialogue (Emanuel, 2001, p. 45). Here too, we'll be thinking about poetry, as an adjunct to our thinking about fathers and father substitutes. We will be looking through a number of lenses here. We change our minds as views evolve. Human development evolves, and so do we. The triangular structure underpins our thinking, as we proceed.

The poet Philip Larkin (2001) (see Chapter 12) knew about what he called the intergenerational haunting, 'deepening like a coastal shelf', and as Cat Stevens said in his song, 'Father and Son', he wasn't listened to, so he had to go away. But people do go on having kids. Is the word 'father' a misnomer, a modern invention? More anon. Father, where art thou?

Children from single-parent families tend to be over-represented in clinic populations. However, this state of family may be no more potentially pathological than the nuclear family, which can become conceptually idealised, and not only within our own cultural milieu. Again, more anon. A 'viable life' as Dilys Daws (1989), psychotherapist and author of *Through the Night*, said, is possible, without a present father or partner. Perhaps it helps again to think about the triangle to examine its relevance as a schema to underpin ideas about fatherhood. Then a paradigm emerges. As I said previously, the triangle, this mathematical construct, figures in some way in all major religions.

The role of the father, or whomever it is on the third point of the triangle, whatever their gender, is vital to the emotional development of the child, internally and thus externally. This topic is approached on three fronts: (1) looking at fathers in myth, iconography and poetry; (2) in clinical work, my own and that of others; and (3) through the lens of classical psychoanalytic thinking. Far from there being a single argument about Fathers, there are as many arguments, perhaps as many as there are fathers, involving philosophy, history, politics and the arts as well as psychoanalysis. As the psychoanalyst Wilfred Bion said, 'psychoanalysis itself is just a stripe on the coat of the tiger' ([1975] 1990). There are no 'proofs' or absolute linkages here. In this way, it may be somewhat different from more academic books offering 'proof', but I hope that anyone reading this text may find it helpful as a way forward, rather in the way of much of Bion's work. As the artist Paul Klee said, if you take a point for a walk, it becomes a line; let's see where we go. Second thoughts, third thoughts are all part of the process of gradual understanding, which forms the ground under our feet. There may be no answers, merely more questions, and each academic and clinician and 'ordinary reader' (is there such a beast?) will hopefully find their own answers. New doors may be opened.

The Native American Leroy Little Bear wrote the Foreword to the physicist David Bohm's book, *On Creativity*, talking of how 'awestruck' he was when reading Bohm's ideas about 'difference' and 'possibilities': that with the aid of 'talking circles', we may all achieve a wider view. As Bohm himself said, what is needed is a 'dialogue' in the real sense of the word, which means 'flowing through' (1996, p. ix).

Fathers in Poetry

This book about fathers and father substitutes ends by thinking about three poems, reflecting on the three-ness that is essential for emotional growth to occur, illustrating the pitfalls as well as the satisfactions of parenting, and particularly of being a father. It was Freud himself who pictured the mind as a poetry-making organ, and it was Bion later who opined that a film or a line from a poem could be more, if not most, helpful in elucidating life's challenges. The paper ends with a quotation from Shakespeare, who so aptly described how the memory of our own fathers lies deep within our minds, and our very bones, affecting the way we parent, be we biological or paternal. We may ignore this at our peril.

There are of course, as I said, independent variables to factor in with each case. Field theory applies here. Each person in the structure, both alive and dead, will affect how the child develops, in an unconscious force field she or he may be unaware of, a labyrinth of possibilities. This was borne out when I was seeing families at the Bishop Harvey Family Service (Edwards & Maltby, 1998). Fathers needed to be strongly encouraged to come to our meetings: they frequently felt they were irrelevant. 'The lives of the human race form a constant plot. We must bear in mind that each person brings a texture of events, environments, other people and other stories will be derived' (Calvino, 1979, p. 92).

As the quantum physicist Carlo Rovelli (2018) asserted: even down to the very smallest items we have at present discovered, quarks, while they may look separate, they are also inextricably bound together. And where I use the word 'fathers', as I have said, partners (male or female partners; he, she or they), co-parents, cisgender, or transgender may be used instead, so we might see the paternal function as being offered by others, regardless of sexual or cultural choices. The 'others' are, as Rovelli suggested, 'inextricably bound together' as those working with families will unpack.

The topic of fathers, then, is a vast one, stretching from macrocosm to microcosm, as each generation hands on to the next, in the human chain. There are fathers as heroes, fathers as villains, ordinary good-enough fathers, some idealised, some denigrated, fathers of daughters, fathers of sons, fathers who walk away (can they be forgiven?), fathers who stay, fathers who form the stuff of fantasy, conscious and unconscious, or fathers who deal with day-to-day reality. What do we remember of our own fathers? What do we want to hand on? What do we not want to hand on? This book is a reflection on that universal theme: Will you be to your father as your father was to you? He may be the hand in the dark, but is this a dark hand, or a light hand, or something that is a mixture of both? You may recognise your own father in these pages, either in the clinical work or in the personal recollections collected here, which may stir you up emotionally, and you may also gain a perspective on other ways of fathering, where culture and cultural assumptions may clash or may meld with individual personal predilections. You may not get to choose your father, biological or not, in any case paternal, but you can construct your own narrative in the universal plot. 'May' perhaps is not the word, you will. This is what one of my contributors said:

> The concept of interviewing people about their fathers reminds me of the story or the American professor of law who was just about to start his lecture to a large crowded lecture hall when the door burst open and a young man rushed in, ran around the hall, fired two shots into

the ceiling and ran out. The professor asked the students what had happened. He received some very varied replies! One bearded man, two brown men, men wearing shorts, men wearing long trousers, three women ... all had fired six shots (rather than two).

They had all witnessed the same event, but minutes afterwards, the number of descriptions of what had happened was probably the square of the number of people in the room. 'That's all you need to know about evidence,' said the professor after the event.

My contributor continued, 'Writing about the relationship with my own father? The question made me think of him as a person in his own right possibly for the first time.'
Too many psychoanalytic books leave out the personal, who we all are, who we might be. Stories bring situations to vibrant life, perhaps as this contributor commented 'possibly for the first time'. These stories may affect your life, presenting as dynamic and vital, as the characters spring to life again in the mind and on the page.

Notes

1 Clinical material has been anonymised and changed to preserve confidentiality while retaining meaning.
2 Psychoanalytic comments by the author are in italics, in brackets and signed JE.

References

Barrows, P. (1995). Oedipal issues at 4 and 44. *Psychoanalytic Psychotherapy*, 9(1), 85–96. https://doi.org/10.1080/02668739500700081
Bion, W. R. (1975/1990). *A memoir of the future*. Routledge.
Bohm, D. (1996). *On creativity*. Routledge.
Brecht, B. (2018). *The collected poems of Bertolt Brecht*, trans. Tom Kuhn and David Constantine. Liveright.
Briggs, A. (2023). Response piece to an article in issue 48.3 of this Journal by Judith Edwards: 'The elusive pursuit of good enough fatherhood, and the single parent family as a modern phenomenon.' *Journal of Child Psychotherapy*, 49(1), 90–94. https://doi.org/10.1080/0075417X.2023.2175229
Calvino, I. (1979). *If on a winter's night a traveler*. Einaudi.
Charmaz, K. (2006). *Constructing grounded theory*. Sage Publications.
Critchlow, K. (1976). *Islamic patterns: An analytical and cosmological approach*. Thames & Hudson.
Daws, D. (1989). *Through the night: Helping parents and sleepless infants*. Free Association Books.
Edwards, J. (2019). *Psychoanalysis and other matters*. Routledge.
Edwards, J., & Maltby, M. (1998). Holding the child in mind: Work with parents and families in a consultation service. *Journal of Child Psychotherapy*, 24(1), 104–133.
Emanuel, R. (2001). On becoming a father – reflections from infant observation. In *The importance of fathers*. Routledge.
The *Guardian* (2023a), Lord's Prayer opening may be 'problematic' says archbishop.

The *Guardian* (2023b), Church of England to consider use of gender-neutral terms for God.
Hofmann, M. (2018). A born contrarian. *The New York Review of Books*, November 29, p. 47.
Jones, K, (2008). The role of the father in psychoanalytic theory. *Studies in Clinical Social Work*, 75(1).
Kraemer, S. (1988) *'The civilisation of fathers'*. Tavistock Public Lecture.
Larkin, P. (2001). This be the verse. In *Collected poems*. Farrar, Straus and Giroux.
Robinson, M. (2014). *Lila*. Virago Press.
Rovelli, C. (2018). *The order of time*. Penguin Books.
Segal, H. (1989). Introduction. In R. Britton, M. Feldman, & E. O'Shaughnessy (eds), *The Oedipus complex today* (pp. 1–10). Karnac.
Tóibín, C. (2018). *Mad, bad, and dangerous to know*. Penguin Books.
Wills, C. (December 9, 2018). Prodigal fathers. *The New York Review of Books*, p. 38.

1 The Idea and Fantasy of the Father Seen Through History

The saccharine song, 'Oh! My Papa' was performed by Eddie Fisher in the 1950s and immortalised by Eddie Calvert with his 'Golden Trumpet'. It captured the hearts of many White western children, including me. We all sat on Papa's knee, as he listened and soothed our troubles away. Deep in our hearts, we crooned alongside Mr Fisher; we miss him so much today. 'O mein Papa' was a nostalgic German song, originally sung by a young woman remembering her beloved, once-famous father, who was a clown, hence her smiling. We may wonder whether the smiles hid tears, as clowns often purportedly tried to do – proponents of eccedentesiast tendencies, as they are called, faking smiles to hide sadness. The song was recorded in English as 'Oh! My Papa' by a number of performers, including the aforementioned Eddie Fisher, whose version was a number one hit in the United States in 1954. Eddie Calvert's version was a number one hit in the United Kingdom, too, and we revelled in the fantasy, even if the reality tended quite frequently to be rather different. We floated effortlessly along, enjoying how we felt, with this image in our minds. It made our lives worth living, even if it contradicted 'reality'. Just as adults after the Second World War might have projected mandalas, a collection of universal forces, symbolising their fears, into flying saucers, as Jung (1959) averred, a modern myth of things seen in the internal sky, and it helped us flow along with what was going on, at least in our fantasies. At the same time, the Belgian surrealist artist Magritte painted his picture of 'raining men' in the external sky, with a background of identical buildings. Were they going to or coming home from work? Hundreds of little identical bowler-hatted, dark-suited men – fathers as they were deemed to be in the late 1960s – rather more involved with their work than with their families. As the poet Edgar Albert Guest (1881–1959) wrote:

> Only a dad with a tired face,
> Coming home from the daily race,
> …
> Merely one of the surging crowd,
> …
> Only a dad, but the best of men.

Only a dad. But if we take a step back, quite a large one, if we go back 6,000 years, a question arises: Is this notion of fatherhood something we have made up, a story to suit our own often rather sentimental predilections? Sebastian Kraemer (1991) in his article, 'The Origins of Fatherhood', looks beyond our human development to the apes that preceded us, where fathers were more random, less selected, and did their own thing rather than hang around after coitus. If they did hold infants, it was for their own protection rather than having anything to do with the infant. Parenting came later, and both parents held a more or less equal role. As Kraemer said:

> Fatherhood was invented by humans during the agricultural revolution about six thousand years ago. Symbolised by the new god-king, it incorporated the mother's originally superior role in primate families: the control or ownership of children. The male deity, it was said, could even make his own offspring without female help. This inflated political figure was designed to compensate for the male's modest role in procreation, once the facts of life were known. (*Patriarchy was perhaps born out of an envious attack on mothers? – JE*)

Before there were humans, there were no fathers. Being a mother was prime. Indeed, in the animal kingdom, females ate their mates after sperm deposit. I recall my own small son, then aged 3, saying with feeling, 'I just realised I can't ever have babies, not even when I'm a grown-up!' The presence of an adult male, preferably friendly, could be an advantage thousands of years ago, but it was not absolutely necessary for the survival of females and infants. Also, it was up to the female with child to choose a male partner, if she had one at all, regardless of the infant's actual paternity. The familiar picture of the exhausted hunter returning with a dead animal to feed his hungry family will have occurred often enough, but his provisions were a bonus, not a necessity. It is quite possible that he would in any case have shared these with his mother and siblings and not with his sexual partner. (*Now there's a new thought – JE*) 'Man the hunter' has for centuries been the unquestioned starting point of human evolution, but this might again have something to do with envy of the capacity to have babies. (*Perhaps we may think about 'toxic masculinity'? – JE*) So there is the syrupy fantasy of the mid-twentieth century, and something more nuanced if we look back. Let's leap forward from 6,000 years ago to the Renaissance to see if things have changed. And what, if anything, remains the same. Are there speaking likenesses here?

In 2006, London's Victoria and Albert Museum put on two Renaissance exhibitions: one about the towering genius of Leonardo Da Vinci (from a little town in northern Italy) and his inventions, and the other about domestic life in the period, 'At Home in Renaissance Italy' – the interior lives of, well, quite affluent folk, but interior nevertheless.

The museum wished to show the private lives of ordinary, predominantly well-to-do people, whose existence revolved, as do our own, around important life events such as birth, marriage (and its potential for a procreative partnership) and death. Sigmund Freud, as is well known, examined Leonardo's life and constructed a psychological picture based on Leonardo's vulture in the cradle dream or fantasy (Freud, 1910), linking this to what he saw as Leonardo's pathological object choice. In the exhibition, 'At Home in Renaissance Italy', within the interior spaces of Renaissance dining halls, kitchens and bedchambers, we see played out the lives of those whose hopes and fears shared much with our own, where ordinary developmental stages were struggled with against the political backdrop of the times. While historians do not usually record these kinds of intimacies, as they deal with broad brush strokes and the ups and downs of political and social periods, it is left to artists and the makers of household and well as 'fine art' artefacts to give us a vivid picture as life as it was lived underneath the broad sweep of history.

I was struck at the beginning of the exhibition to come upon two portraits, one of a man with his son, and the second of his wife with her daughter, placed side by side. Touchingly, these portraits were reportedly separated hundreds of years ago and were brought together for the first time in this exhibition: gazes were re-united. Each tells a story, and together they offer us a picture of a family, idealised perhaps, but where one can without difficulty read something about aspirations and struggles, fears and dangers as well as desire for status and recognition in their world. As the reviewer in the *Guardian* of 7 October 2006 commented, they introduce us to 'the competing narratives at the heart of the Renaissance: ostentatious display, acquisitiveness, lineage, humanity'. It is possibly the humanity that particularly drew so many people, as was reported, and I think these two portraits offer us a study in humanity as the two children can be seen to be responding in different ways to the challenges of the Oedipus complex (as outlined here) and its resolution. Both are latency age, or approaching it – with the boy, whom the curator comments looks 'quite timid', possibly the older. The little girl looks out from behind her mother, whose protective hand rests on her shoulder. The child looks straight at the artist, as if she has somehow made her transition from mother as love object to mother as object for identification. Her mother carries the fur of a marten, thought to protect women from the dangers of childbirth (a 20% mortality rate is noted, so far removed from our own current European statistic of 0.0001%). The marten was thought to conceive through the ear and give birth by mouth – a process concretely far removed from the real travails of childbirth.

Father and son present what might be seen as a rather different story. While the real and palpable danger for women was childbirth, for men in an age where people lived and died quite frequently by the sword, the large rapier carried by father (which made men adopt a particular way of walking to accommodate its bulk) is a symbol of sexual and physical power. Okay, it's a large penis substitute. The little boy does indeed look timid and uncertain – his father holds the boy's left hand with his ungloved right hand, and the boy is also holding tightly to his father's arm with his own right hand, looking

The Idea and Fantasy of the Father Seen Through History 15

uncertainly over at the mother, while the father himself looks out at the artist. The boy has his own little rapier, but his cloak is still lined with ermine, like his mother's. One could think about the uncertainties shown here of the transition from mother to father as an object for identification, and the boy's unconscious ambivalence, as he still shelters underneath his mother's cloak in his mind, about the father who looks so powerful, and who is one half of the strong parental couple, which he will have fully to acknowledge, internally and externally, in order to progress.

This is an exhibition packed with interest for us, with details regarding birth, childrearing (with an actual sixteenth-century baby-walker) and family being then, as now, so crucial for personality development. This couple could be seen to represent what is often missing for the deprived children who child psychotherapists tend to see now, those children who someone recently called 'urban warriors', who have lived without internal protection to defend against tenderness and dependence, and who live in impoverished and bleak internal worlds.

And here are the comments of a doctor, a general practitioner, recording the baby's observations of his father:

> I had not expected to enjoy the Infant Observation module as much as I have. As a GP, I have carried out innumerable examinations on children as well as hundreds of newborn and six-week-old infant checks. While doing these, I am used to noting the colour and condition of their skin, the presence or absence of facial expression or eye movements, any limb activity and so on. Some infants glow and some are pale and wan, some seem happy and others grizzle. As one examines and handles them, they all feel so very different and individual. I may be aware of restlessness, passivity, being accommodated and wilfully resisted. But without fail, I come away from an infant examination feeling that I have briefly met an individual. Infant Observation is quite different. First of all, there is no gain of intimacy from touch, movement or direct interaction. The infant is observed from a distance, and the family style must be respected. One must obtrude as little as possible between the baby and the family. At first, I found this strange but soon realised that I had to rely on my wits and senses in a different way to assess what was going on. In being aware of how he is held and treated, of his tiny movements and gestures, I have found that I conceptualise 'my' infant's immediate life in a way that I had not, either as a father or a GP. I am aware that I am not scoring his health or development but simply watching and sharing in it. I now feel his helplessness, his pleasures and disappointments and occasionally feel what his skin and muscles must feel when he is held in certain ways. I guess a little at how wonderful feeding, his mother's voice or some music must seem to him, and I wonder about the times when he seems to communicate but is not heard or noticed. A poignant moment occurred in one of my early observations when the

baby was being held awkwardly and horizontally in his father's arms. He looked with great concentration up at his father's face while his father talked about him to visitors. His gaze remained fixed and imploring for a long time, and eventually, his proud father glanced at him briefly before carrying on with his conversation – and still the baby looked up at his father's face with hope and expectation. After a time, his gaze and expression changed and quietened so that I felt a moment had been lost forever. I know that I felt so much on his behalf and wished his need had been recognised and held. It made me think about being a 'good enough' parent and what it means to be a 'good enough' child. I realise that I am getting to know this baby from how his life is, and I enjoy the struggle of making sense of this experience, and writing it up each week. All very different from the insights of a busy GP. Finally, I can quietly reflect upon this intense and personal experience, on how my own infancy might have been and on how all this can be related over time to Freud, Klein, Bion and Winnicott. A new, different and rich experience, which I wish that I had had before.

References

Freud, S. (1910). Leonardo da Vinci: A psychosexual study of an infantile reminiscence. Available at: mindsplain.com/wp-content/uploads/2020/08/…

Jung, C. G. (1959). *Flying saucers: A modern myth of things seen in the skies*. Psychology Press.

Kraemer, S. (1991). The origins of fatherhood. *Family Process, 30,* 377–392.

2 Having a Father and Being a Father

Hamlet's relationship with his dead father is one that springs to mind. In Shakespeare's play, *Hamlet*, the relationship between Hamlet and his father, King Hamlet, is a pivotal element of the play. This relationship is characterised by deep respect, admiration and a strong sense of duty. Hamlet holds his father in high esteem, often reminiscing about King Hamlet's virtues and his excellence as a ruler. This is evident in Hamlet's comparisons between his father and his uncle Claudius. For instance, Hamlet describes his father as a figure of great nobility and valour, contrasting sharply with his disdain for Claudius, whom he sees as morally corrupt and inferior. (*Perhaps this is a version of the Oedipus Complex? – JE*) The appearance of King Hamlet's ghost sets the main plot in motion, as it reveals the truth about his murder and charges Hamlet with the duty of avenging his death. Hamlet's relationship with his father thus becomes the driving force behind his actions throughout the play. The ghost's command profoundly affects Hamlet, causing him to struggle with the moral and existential implications of revenge. Hamlet's grief over his father's death is profound and genuine, showing the depth of his loyalty. This grief is exacerbated by his mother Gertrude's quick remarriage to Claudius, which Hamlet sees as a betrayal of his father's memory. (*So perhaps not an Oedipal issue here – JE*) Hamlet's mourning clothes and his reflections on the transient nature of life and death further illustrate his deep sorrow and ongoing connection to his father. Hamlet's identity is closely tied to his father's legacy. He frequently compares himself to his father, grappling with feelings of inadequacy and the heavy burden of living up to King Hamlet's reputation. This sense of legacy drives Hamlet's actions and his contemplation of life, death and what it means to honour his father's memory.

Overall, the relationship between Hamlet and his father is central to the themes of loyalty, revenge and the search for truth and justice in the play. It shapes Hamlet's motivations and actions, ultimately leading to the tragic conclusion. Hamlet himself, of course, does not go on to become a father and pass on these qualities he so admires, but we do have Shakespeare's own relationship to his own son. William Shakespeare's relationship with his son Hamnet is a subject of historical speculation and rather limited documented evidence. Hamnet Shakespeare was born in 1585 and was one of Shakespeare's three children, alongside his twin sister Judith and their older sister Susanna. Hamnet died at the age of 11 in 1596, a death that profoundly affected Shakespeare.

Shakespeare's works do not directly reference Hamnet, but some scholars suggest that his grief over Hamnet's death may have influenced what he wrote. For example, the play *Hamlet*, written a few years after Hamnet's death, shares an almost similar name and explores themes of loss and mourning.

Shakespeare spent much of his time in London, while his family lived in Stratford-upon-Avon, which might suggest a physical distance. However, this was not uncommon for the time and doesn't necessarily indicate an emotional distance. The few surviving records hint at a traditional father-son relationship, but the depth of their emotional connection remains largely unknown due to the scant personal documents from Shakespeare's life. We can only conjecture.

Having a Father: Contributors' Views

Having a father – a multifaceted issue – gave some of my potential contributors pause for much thought indeed, as one said, he had 'never thought about' his father as a person with his own history. Let's continue, why not, with the burden of attachment to tyrannical objects. This text below is quoted by kind permission of Anne Alvarez, retired lecturer at the Tavistock Clinic:

> In Hilary Mantel's (2005) *The Mirror and the Light*, Thomas Cromwell is writing in his own notebook, *The Book of Henry* (393), giving advice to his son, his nephew and his beloved chief clerk, Rafe, on how to manage while not displeasing, omnipotent and tyrannical rulers. He tells them not to flatter but to find something the king really did do to deserve praise, otherwise he will know you are simply flattering him. It is clear that Cromwell recognises the narcissism and the dangerousness in the king but wishes to pass on the skills he has learned and the tools he has acquired, i.e., those which have enabled him to manipulate the king into choosing more rational and successful ways of running the kingdom. The King tends to take Cromwell's advice, but is always encouraged to think it was all his own idea. Yet Mantel never lets us think that Cromwell, although he is wise to the flaws in his master, either hates or despises him. Why? We know from Volume 1 of the trilogy, *Wolf Hall*, that Cromwell as a boy had to flee England after the thousandth murderous attack by his drunken and brutal blacksmith father which this time nearly killed him. He came back years later from Italy and Germany, an educated, wealthy and hugely competent man, and his wisdom and brilliance in managing finance and the law of the land, led him to rise through the ranks to become the king's closest adviser and enabler. To the very end he was loyal, even in the Tower awaiting his execution.

There are one or two admiring mentions of his father's physical strength near the end of the book – did he still love him, and did he still love Henry? Although the Cromwell of the novel may be a highly fictionalised character, the tendency to remain afflicted by, yet still dependent on bad parental objects is a familiar story in our clinical work. When it can become addictive and perverse too.

Juliet Hopkins, another lecturer at the Tavistock, was attending the seminars to get a taste of my Kleinian take on theory. She herself is in the Independent Group, and a distinguished Winnicottian (see Horne & Lanyado, 2005). She asked, 'Why do you have to call that addiction?' and added that Joseph Sandler had pointed out that a woman may choose violent men who remind her of her father because, despite the violence, she may have had an attachment to him. That which is familiar, can also, even if it is at times cruel, be dear to us. Familiarity breeds contempt, but it may breed affection too. Maybe the abusive father was the one who gave the woman breakfast every morning. In any case, whatever we call this, bond or bondage, it is very hard for some people to get a distance from and perspective on their internal objects, even if they have managed to escape the actual external ones, by physical separation, or the death of the parent. As we all know, those superego figures can sit on our shoulders for decades – *indeed they can*.

Alvarez continues:

> And they can carry deadly power in a variety of ways. John Le Carré's character, Magnus Pym's father Rick, in *A Perfect Spy* is relinquished externally but refuses to keep his distance and Magnus is regularly tormented by his intrusive appearances. Magnus ends up filled with ever more shame, not only on behalf of his con-man father, but because of his own identification with him and the damage to his own character. It is a bleak book, but also full of love – mainly for his Czech opposite number for whom he betrays his country in their spy game but also, mixed with horrible fascination, I think, for his reprehensible father. He writes, 'But even while I fawned on you and exchanged radiant smiles with you and bolstered you in your idiotic schemes, I knew that you had pulled the best con of them all. You were nothing any more. Your mantle had passed to me, leaving you a naked little man, and myself the biggest con I knew.' When his father finally dies, he is free to kill himself.

Le Carré (personal communication) said to JE that this was based on memories of his own father, and yet as a father himself he could write to his one of his four sons, Tim:

> My love for you is undivided and strangely, or not so strangely, I feel close to you and the pains you have endured (a mental health condition).

I love your courage and your moral decency, your questing brain, your uncompromising soul and your lovely wit.' He talked of their being 'companions in solitude.

His bipolar son had a life that ended abruptly when he was 59, and he died of a pulmonary embolism. I like to think that were David Cornwell (aka John Le Carré) still living, he would have written with eloquence about what he wished to pass on, and what not. And yet perhaps in these words above, to his son, and to 'Rick Pym', he has.

A slightly different form of 'bad' paternal object, kindly, but so depressed that it produced a dampening effect on everyone, can also have a damaging effect.

Alvarez says:

We still have much to learn of the craft of psychoanalysis, and I will leave the last word to the late Hilary Mantel, even though it concerns the usage of words not silences (Mantel, 2005, p. 568). This is Cromwell thinking about the king's view of Sir Thomas Wyatt, the poet and diplomat. 'The king knows Wyatt's uses. He is able to read sighs. Construe by contraries. His word is just what a diplomat's word should be: as clear as glass and as unstable as water.' I would add that when we try to understand somebody else's mind, we are really travelling in another country and diplomacy is more important in psychoanalytic work than we might think. (*As clear as glass, as unstable as water ... this diplomatic advice could be useful for us all – JE*)

Let's carry on with the classic picture of a powerful, omnipotent father, epitome of Freud's superego, who then ends up in his son's mind being 'suffused by light'. In the 1880s, Richard Jefferies, the nature writer and journalist, wrote his *The Story of My Heart*, which was panned as being 'speculatively spiritual' at the time (Jefferies, 1883). And yet, if we think about our memories of our father, perhaps they do indeed morph into something more ineffable. Jefferies would lie on the clifftop above Beachy Head, running the friable pebbles through his hands, seeing them as 'receptacles of ancient sunlight' (Wroe, 2016, p. 12). Our memories do indeed suffer 'a sea change' ... it is a moving and heartfelt process, when it succeeds ... do we consider this as a 'vaseline on the lens' phenomenon, or does it strike us in a more profound way, joining the numinous if fleeting thoughts inside our minds?

Here below we have MY FATHER in capital letters ... clearly someone from a classy background, Rolls Royce and all:

In my mind, I have two clear images of my father that come from black and white photographs. The first, taken by a professional photographer shows a man, his hands folded in front of him, leaning on a mahogany desk, wearing a sharkstooth Huntsman suit, a smart tie, a checked shirt, dark eyebrows, large nose, set jaw, hair parted and slicked back, staring out of the picture with confident eyes; a picture of power, status, and control. Behind him is a painting of the cliffs between Eastbourne and Dover painted in greys and grey-greens, a mixture of natural formations and coastal concrete defences. The look on my father's face and the sense of both permanence and defence against the vicissitudes of nature bounce from one to the other.

A superego figure indeed. According to Freud's structural model of the mind, as expressed in *The Ego and the Id* (1923), the superego is the part of the mind that comprises internalised moral standards and ideals learned both from parents and society – our sense of right and wrong.

I have had trouble with my father, which has been all to do with power: Father, Son and Holy Ghost. (*The triangle here is condensed into one powerful figure – JE*) His authority – which was physical, he was a big man and was backed up by a number of systems, not least by the love and companionship of my mother – was absolute and based on the Catholic religion of his childhood that meted out reward and punishment. He seemed in his judgements and rewards to be doing, as he thought himself, the work of a divine authority. (*Can we think of this as being a product of a particular time, or the cultural assumptions made in the white western world before the advent of same-sex parenting? – JE*)

When I think about him, I think of his physical bulk, his barrel chest, his booming voice, the way he smelled of Victor aftershave and Roger & Gallet sandalwood soap, his well-tended nails, his gold and jade cufflinks, his Church's shoes and his Rolls-Royces. He taught me how to drive by sitting me on his lap and driving round and round a seaside car park until I felt somehow under his overriding control to be in control of this enormous car while sitting in the lap of an enormous man. (*Here, we can see Alvarez's idea about imitation preceding identification – JE*)

On Sunday mornings, he would take his three postwar boys onto Hampstead Heath, setting various tasks, as we walked or raced each other towards Jack Straws Castle pub: who will be first to bring him a stick with three branches, a four-leafed clover, a leaf with three points? Who can climb this bank, 'Everest', fastest? Smith's crisps and Cherry-ade were awarded to the winners. He was a great storyteller, and often after Sunday lunch, we would all climb into bed and he would tell us stories in which we were all protagonists, protecting the crown jewels or discovering treasures on mysterious islands in the north. He was demanding if fun when on holiday. He liked his boats, his horses, his golf – he liked to win, he liked to sail to the horizon and he liked to sail just for the fun of being out there. It was he who made sure that each of us as children had a boat. He introduced us to that metaphor for self-determination and being 'ship-shape'.

My dad introduced me to Piero Della Francesca. A reproduction on board of a Fra Angelico annunciation was always on our 'boys bedroom' wall. My love of *The Baptism of Christ* at the National Gallery – which remains for me one of the most mysterious and wonderful paintings with its lucid skies, utter silence and held breath, the angel that looks out towards us and includes us in this moment; the drop, held in the small dish that seems to contain and demand our attention – I owe to him.

He was generous but also absolute in his expectation of performance. Whether it was the declension of Latin verbs or the cooking of the soup, everything had to be right. I vividly remember the embarrassment when 'Nurse', our nanny, retained as cook to the household after we came down from the nursery to share meals with our parents, was made to cry when sand was found in the watercress soup. When dining at Wheelers or at Chez Antoine, the cook was brought to the table to be complimented on the sauce for the turbot.

Daddy, when present, was very present, but even when absent, he was there. Seeing him off was a family affair. Like God, his authority was to be seen in everyone and his agents were minion. I was sent away to school. He was always leaving and writing postcards, if not whole letters, from faraway places including instructions on schooling. Every master, whether of horse-riding, ballroom dancing, rugby, French or religious instruction, was an agent. He liked to sort things out, and I – we – were things to be sorted out.

With his chauffeurs, secretaries and agents worldwide, he could both make things happen to us and around us. If I am making him sound omnipresent, omniscient, absent a lot of the time – except in relatively rare moments of close physical contact – that would be absolutely correct.

'*Lavorare est orari*' – work is prayer – was a familiar refrain. We were here on Earth for a purpose and had to fulfil that purpose to do God's work. Work was definitely 90% perspiration and 10% inspiration. Where did he get all this from? Probably his Marist Brothers education in their abbey school in Scotland, reinforced by his time both as an infantryman, a tank corps officer, and all his experiences in the ghastliness of the Western Front. He was a survivor, not just of the Somme and Ypres but of a highly contested home life. His parents, unusual for the time, separated. His father, a successful vintner, returned to Ireland, while my paternal grandmother retired to Stratford-Upon-Avon. He was the only member of a five-child family to marry and spent a great deal of his time looking after the affairs of his brothers and sisters. (*This experience of the Somme, somewhat glossed over here, is in stark contrast to the experience of the father of one of my colleagues: he had been one of those detailed to bury the dead after the Somme catastrophe. He never spoke about it afterwards. It was locked inside him – JE*)

The second image I hold of my father is a pale, slightly over-exposed photograph that I took of him myself while we were on a short retreat together at Quarr Abbey on the Isle of Wight, many years after that first photograph. His hair is now white, he is looking down and smiling ruefully, his arms are crossed, he is wearing a cardigan and a Viyella shirt. He looks as strong as ever but now softer, as if amusingly considering something maybe previously thought less worthy of his attention. I like to think of him now like this – suffused by light and less in control, more prepared to take things as they come, to take me as I came to be, but he went before that entirely happened. 'Suffused by light': A moving recollection, a sea change indeed. It was Johann Wolfgang Goethe, Germany's foremost and formidable poet-scientist, who shouted 'Mehr Licht!' ('More Light') as he lay dying, and it was Einstein who approached the conclusion that light and truth were one (Wroe, 2016, p. 117). While Herbert wrote that any person could be blinded by 'any glitt'ring look', we might also conjecture, as did Melanie Klein, that our memories of our parents could be transformed over time. This is a vital aspect to bear in mind: we can change, our memories can change.

Years can go by, as this story below shows, before any sort of 'closure' is reached – if it ever can be. This father is described as a riddle, wrapped in a mystery:

It is a long time since I was asked what my father was like, or how I feel about him - let alone put this down in writing. It is now 20 years since his death, and 20 years plus a further one year since my mother's own departure. It took several decades after leaving parental care (by becoming an undergraduate a long way from home) to achieve some sort of 'closure', or permanent internal settlement concerning my thoughts and feelings about my parents – most especially my father. This task, achieving 'settlement' within my own self, included several periods of psychotherapy, and an underlying leitmotif within my life from mid-adolescence to late middle age. It was also formative to my vocational direction (Psychologist, then Psychotherapist and finally a grief counsellor). Once this resolution was eventually embraced, I was able to relate to each of them face-to-face in an unconditional loving, compassionate and respectful way. In my mother's case, this was achieved far more easily, and a great many years prior to my father.

However, by this writing I have discovered, to my surprise, that I have of late been procrastinating. So, to break this impasse, I know full well I need to find a keyhole, and just get going. Ergo I ask, 'What is the strongest memory from childhood or early adolescence which remains both vivid and clear to this day and connects me with my father in some direct way?' In so doing, an event leaps to mind and revealingly, it is a memory of an incident wherein Geoffrey, my dad, is entirely absent. No more procrastination now.

Geoffrey was very different from other fathers – this was the standard reaction of my young friends when they met him and was usually expressed in direct contrast to their own father. It was, as far as I can remember, pretty well always meant as a positive comment. They found him interesting, and I liked that. He was not present for much of the time during my first 8 years or so, doing shift work – but that was probably normal for most fathers in our community back then – not really that different, so my early conceptualisation of him as unconventional must also have been dependent on some of the reactions or perceptions by salient adult figures in my early years who, as far as I can remember, did seem to appreciate and value him. I can recall my maternal grandfather Jim saying to me (with attendant Yorkshire accent): 'Your father is right peculiar, but e's a good lad – 'e doesn't drink, swear or disrespect women, right respectful, just a tad odd. There ain't now't as queer as folk ye know.' In other words, he was just human, but very much in his own way. I liked the fact that he was eccentric. The strongest difference or distinction I can remember from a very early age was the fact that he did not eat meat, whereas my mother did. Meals always had a non-meat component, but when affordable, my mother would also present an additional meat option, but not for him. Geoffrey did not require me to imitate his vegetarian regime – he was clear that such dietary preferences or principles should not be imposed on others – as it had been in his case. Furthermore, he never used physical means to promote 'discipline' (as in his case), and he usually preferred to explain, or actually demonstrate the right action. The norm for my extended family, my peers, my neighbourhood, school and undoubtedly much of society at this time was dependent on the principle of not 'spoiling the rod'. Physical punishment was the norm. This particular paternal eccentricity did not sit too well with my mother, when, inevitably, my actions fell short of her own expectations of me. He would say, and I can remember this clearly (no doubt because it was a tremendous relief to hear it said under the particular circumstances): 'If our son ever does something as bad or worse than I have done, then I will punish him.' My friends found this to be utterly incredible. I thought it made amazing good sense (as well as a most welcome intervention), and an example of my father's excellence. I considered myself most fortunate. Geoffrey was a fitness fanatic who followed the 'Charles Atlas' Body Building Programme, as well as a champion swimmer in his school days, which included competing for his school, City and County (he met my mother in a swimming pool during a swimming competition where she was also a participant). Crucially for me, in so far as my future scholastic and intellectual development is concerned, he was a great reader, eclectic in taste and extensive in breadth. I was fortunate in that I grew up in a house full of books – lots of them. I particularly remember there being many history books, including history of science as well as science-based texts with associated philosophical themes. Part of Geoffrey's collection included the work of many classic science fiction and fantasy writers – Jules Verne, H. G. Wells, Edgar Allan Poe, Conan Doyle and Rider Haggard – and I had read a good proportion of the written output of these authors by the time I was 11 or 12. Geoffrey had what I consider to be a great sense of humour. My mother did not share this appreciation, nor did many of his peers I noticed. It underpinned my developing appreciation of the emergent post-war BBC Radio comedy trend unfolding at the time: The Goons, Beyond Our Ken, The Navy Lark, Hugh and I, Hancock's Half Hour and the like. Offbeat, anarchic, tongue in cheek and totally irreverent. The one thing that remains true of my own behaviour to this day, pure Geoffrey, is that same sense of humour. This remains something of him that I am delighted to preserve and practise. He was also very practical and competent in a DIY fashion; he built a fitted kitchen in our first home at a time when there was no such thing as a 'flat pack'. Both my parents did home decorations when this was also atypical. Like most of his peers, he was interested and knowledgeable about cars and motor bikes with associated mechanical skills. However, little of the foregoing really says much about what he means to me and what impact he had on my own development as a person, as opposed to a long list of behaviours, skills, quirks or talents. It still remains open as to what kind of person he was. As a person. So back to my most salient early memory: An Unexpected Event of Major Importance ... I was staying at my grandparents' (Nancy and Jim) for a few weeks when I was around 15 years of age. I was with them because my parents were away in London (the reasons for this London stay did not become known to me for some years later – described below). It was great for me to be with them. The first six years of my early childhood had been spent in their household, as my parents lived with them toward the end of the war (and until the post-war housing construction programme resulted in affordable homes becoming available and affordable for them and others). As I write, I clearly remember J walking towards me across their backyard, slowly, purposefully – and sensing he had something on his mind, something important, and it had something to do with me. It did feel something bad must have happened, or was about to happen, and maybe I was in trouble?

I remember him saying (again in his Yorkshire dialect), 'There is summat ye need to see. Cumon, lad, lets ger off.' Instead of the usual route he and my father always took when heading towards the usual destinations, Jim turned off into a part of our own immediate neighbourhood, new to me. I clearly remember wondering why I had never been to this part of Sheffield before, all within a mile or so from where we had always lived. When we approached the end of the built-up area, the road came to a dead end. We were now beside a long, high sooty black sandstone wall with a pair of similarly blackened stone pillars framing a black wrought iron gate, which we opened with some difficulty. Inside was a large, wild, dense overgrown garden. A few blackened stone crosses and the odd scruffy-looking angel emerged here and there: it was an abandoned cemetery. J stopped at the end of the enclosed area, and I strove to get a glimpse of what he was looking at. It was just a small oblong clearing, freshly cleared and well weeded, enclosed within an oppressive tangle of overgrowth. I remember there being some freshly planted flowers and having the impression that someone had recently tried to make a little garden, within a small oblong patch of freshly raked earth. For a while there was silence, before Jim said, 'I did this, I was 'ere all day yesterday.' Then, after another pause, he said, 'Does tha know 'o this is?' 'No.' I had no idea to whom he referred. Total blank. 'This is where your brother is. Stuart. Buried here. This is his grave.' I don't recall saying anything, but I do remember him saying, 'It's about time you knew where he is, you are old enough to know.' We stood there, me incredulous and dumb, before Jim eventually said, 'I come 'ere every now an then, I tidy up and mek sure 'e is not forgotten. Your Nan and I feel it's 'bout time yer knew. Y'er old enough now.' I do not recall what I said, if anything.

It had been some years since I had stopped asking the question, 'Where has Stuart gone? Why hasn't he come home, where is he?' It was Jim who, 8 years since I last saw Stuart, told me where he was – in the Bole Hills. Alone, but not it seems, completely forgotten. Stuart had died of pneumonia when I was 8 and he was 7. I think I last saw him when I was 7. He had suffered massive cerebral palsy at birth (blind, no mobility, breathing difficulties, swallowing impairment, etc.), arising from a brain injury as a result of medical malpractice. My parents, Geoffrey and Dorothy, were 21 and 22 years old, respectively, when he was born, which was only shortly before we were evicted from the house owned by my paternal grandfather Horace (my paternal grandmother Christine had given my parents this house as a wedding gift, but Christine died shortly after the gifting – as the result of an air raid – and crucially just prior to her completing the legal process. My grandfather chose not to honour her wishes by denying it was a gift.) So my parents moved in with my maternal grandparents. We – that is my parents, myself and Stuart – lived with Nancy and Jim for the next 5 or 6 years, before my parents eventually moved into their own house. In retrospect, I believe this move was the critical factor in Stuart going into state care – as my mother could not have been able to provide the same high level of care for Stuart (plus looking after me) on her own as a result of uprooting from her parents' home. I remember learning from my mother many years later that his feeding regime would take hours per meal because his spasticity severely affected his swallowing. It was more than a full-time job. During our early period of communal living, my dad worked extra shifts in the steel works (saving for a deposit for their own home), which also meant I did not see as much of him during my first 8 years as I did in the years following. My maternal grandparents accordingly had an especially strong connection with me, especially so due to my mother's primary focus on Stuart, and my father's work pattern. I did not have any contact with my paternal grandfather as a result of this eviction action; my father continued to have some limited intermittent contact, but only at weddings or funerals for my mother. I refused to go to his funeral when I was in my 30s (although both my parents did). My brother Stuart was not expected to live for more than a few days or weeks following his traumatic birth, but the epic care my mother provided meant he lived for as long as he did. By the time he was nearly seven, my mother was persuaded by the GP to transfer his care to the NHS (then in its own infancy; it had just started to create residential care facilities for severely disabled children in the region). My mother had resisted this move for some time because she rightly feared he would suffer if not given the same level of quality care that she provided. As feared, Stuart's health declined rapidly after this care handover took place, and he soon became very ill. He died within a few months of the transfer to state care (from pneumonia) – alone and separated from his mother and the rest of us. Some people thought this was a good thing at that time. I was not told Stuart was going into someone else's care when he left home for the last time, nor that he that had died. Obviously, I never went to his funeral. I was simply told, when I periodically raised the question of his whereabouts, that he had 'gone to live with Jesus'. There was no talk and no sharing of this loss and the emotional burden therein. It was a forbidden zone, and I soon learnt not to ask about him. I actually thought during this time that Jesus was a real person, living in secret somewhere in or Sheffield, and definitely not a good person to stay with. Dorothy subsequently experienced severe depression and went into hospital care herself. She was given electric shock treatment ('electroconvulsive therapy', to put it politely), which did not help her and, in due course, was being considered for prefrontal lobotomy. During these years of in-patient psychiatric care I did visit her, presumably when she felt able to see me (in other words, not often or regularly), and I have (as I write) clear memories of her ward and her incarcerated peers who were also receiving shock treatment, as well as those who were recovering from a lobotomy. This was not nice to witness, but I knew my visits were important for both of us and looked forward to them. The reason my parents were away in London at the time Jim took me on that trip to the Bole Hills was because my dad had come to the conclusion that my mother was not only not healing, but actually deteriorating in the psychiatric hospital where she had been an inpatient off and on for 2–3 years. That Dorothy was being considered for prefrontal surgery terrified her, and he was becoming desperate in turn. As it so happened during this time of heightened anxiety about my mum's mental health, in his reading and searching for alternatives, my dad came across the work of someone called L. Ron Hubbard, an American author who claimed to have founded a new psychology and therapeutic approach to mental ill health. My dad wrote to Hubbard to ask for advice and help and was told a new 'clinic' had recently opened in London, so he booked a place for himself and Dorothy. He went to the psychiatric hospital where Dorothy was an in-patient and against the very strong opposition of the clinical staff discharged her and took her to London. The outcome of all this was highly positive for Dorothy, but over time, it became negative for my father. In my mother's case, she made a rapid recovery following this new treatment in London and did not experience any further in-patient psychiatric care. She had further children, eventually acquired and successfully ran her own business (a hotel) and was inclined to hire staff who had a history of mental illness (in most cases with a positive outcome). She did not think highly of the Hubbard therapy; however, she did say to me (by the time I was an adult) that this period in London was indeed fundamental to her recovery. Later, when pressed about what was the one critical factor in her recovery, she said it was because Geoffrey had 'stood up' for her. By this she meant he had taken direct action of his own accord and had removed her from danger (the psychiatric hospital). She felt safe, protected and cherished. My father, on the other hand, felt it was the Hubbard treatment that was the key to her cure. Consequently, he remained under the influence of the Scientology movement for many years thereafter, frequently getting into arguments with those who were either sceptical or actively opposed to the movement. I was probably the principal person with whom he debated Scientology and the credibility of L. Ron Hubbard. The fact Jim had introduced me to the truth as to Stuart's whereabouts meant I soon began to ask questions about the past again. It was no longer 'where is he?' – which neither Geoffrey nor Dorothy had been able to face – but about the 'back story'. I gradually learnt about their early struggles for the first time: the devastation of the injuries Stuart experienced at birth;

the conventional wisdom that these things should not be talked about, allied with the deep superstition that still held strong in those days that such things were an act of God (and not medical incompetence); the selfish cruelty of my father's father, in contrast with the compassion of certain relatives and friends; and (probably most disturbingly for me) the incredible innocence of my father – his naivety had meant he had not challenged the foregoing threats or challenges – most especially his father, but in effect had complied with the eviction. Similarly, the entry into in-patient care by my mother. Above all, he was the one most inclined to avoid talking about Stuart and his death (hence my grandfather taking me to the cemetery when he did). He had (understandably, under the circumstances of the time) encouraged my mother (or at least had not sought to discourage her) to go where she feared, indeed dreaded, namely the local 'Looney Bin' as they were then called. He had complied with conventional wisdom concerning mental illness, until of course he came across L. Ron Hubbard. He had not acted badly, but I concluded by the time I left home that he had conformed, and I wished that he had not. The riddle that persisted for me seemingly for an aeon was that he had appeared to me to be so different, that is, non-conforming. The impact of Stuart's birth and subsequent death seems to have paralysed this admirable part of him – until, that is, his encounter with Scientology. The flip side of this positive event was he remained under Hubbard's influence for much too long before eventually becoming 'reformed', so to speak. I believe my gentle but persistent process of enquiry concerning the life and death of Stuart, which was activated by my trip to the Bole Hills, meant that my mother did eventually begin to grieve, more than 8 years after his death, and 16 years after his birth.

Talking, reflecting, assessing, affirming, sharing, reliving, crying, laughing, celebrating, hugging. Eventually, this culminated in Dorothy accepting that she had done an incredible job. Heroic indeed. That she was not to blame for his injuries or his death. That she had made the right (only?) choice in handing over care, *under the circumstances*. That the new home and a new life were justified (essential). In all, it took nearly 50 years before she could actually begin to celebrate Stuart's life. It was only then that my father followed suit. I had no idea that my trip with Jim to the Bole Hills would mean that my vocational direction thereafter would become psychological research (I did a PhD in Psychology); leading into innovative services for adults and children with learning disabilities; in turn working and teaching in the field of counselling/psychotherapy; then latterly (and finally) grief therapy. Nor that it would not be until my mother had died that my father could allow himself to fully grieve. For many years, he would leave the room whenever my mother and I started to talk about Stuart. Many times, Dorothy and I would find ourselves talking about it precisely because he was elsewhere. She was the parent who had a diagnosis of 'depression', but my father undoubtedly also carried this with (and perhaps for) her, then later continued or maintained it for many years after her. I think it was my dad who was probably the most incapacitated by Stuart's death at the time it occurred, becoming the one who more than any other at the time completely contained the grief by denying that the death could or should be talked about. The grief became fossilised. However, if sorrow be denied words, then 'The grief that dare not Speak knits up the o-er wrought heart, and bids it break.' And it did. I am not sure about writing about my own father. My father was deeply scarred by his war experiences and found talking about anything emotional really difficult; this was not uncommon in those times. I am a completely different father, and almost have a negative identification with him rather than feeling he passed much on about being a father. The one thing that he did was to have a strong sense of justice and ethical behaviour, but this too came with too much superego contamination. Unfortunately, my analytic experience seemed to confirm this, and it is only in later years when I have had intensive short-term dynamic psychotherapy (and still am having it) that have I managed to really free myself more from a more guilt-induced way of being in the world that I think my father bequeathed me.

Here is another recollection, of an old dad, 'old enough to be your grandfather'! Is this another riddle?

My father was born in December 1896; I was born in October 1944. So he was an old dad, even by the mores of the time. For some reason, he never let me forget that. 'I'm old enough to be your grandfather', he would bellow. I could never see what point he was trying to make – except perhaps to reinforce his dominance. As an aside, my own son was born in 1993, so I became a father at almost exactly the same age as my dad. But it never occurred to me to even think of, let alone express, such a sentiment.

But that remark set the scene for our relationship. He was an old man and looked it.

He had been shot up in the WWI trenches and was whisked back to London on a hospital train, aged under 20. More than once, he told me the story that, as he was lying on a stretcher on Paddington Station, a nurse leant over him murmuring: 'The ambulance won't be much longer, old man.' He was hospitalised for six months, as nurses first removed bits of shattered bone from his leg, and then waited for the leg to heal (no antibiotics or bionic implants in those days, of course). He left hospital on crutches, never fully recovering, and always walking with a stick. So, at a very young age, he was the very picture of senility: an image, in retrospect, I suspect he rather enjoyed.

So, from my earliest years, I remember my father as a self-identifying old man. However, our relationship was not one of benign grandfather doting on wide-eyed grandson. It was more of mild disciplinarian exerting control over a young boy, using advanced age to bolster his status.

So I was always slightly terrified of him: as indeed was my mother, as she later confided. Nevertheless, he was generous enough to spare time from his work (he was a novelist, with nearly 40 titles to his name), playing card games with me in the holidays from boarding school. We also played a game called Chinese Checkers, which I remember often winning at age 12. After his death, my mother told me he used to get really angry that I had trounced him. Funny reaction: if my own son had displayed such cognitive muscle, I would have been delighted.

Dad was a great raconteur, with many admirers in the club he belonged to. He often invited me there, giving me fizzy lemonade to drink, as I was underage. He would say, 'I'm looking forward to the day when I can buy you a drink, boy.' That day never came, as he died when I was 16. Curiously, I found myself shedding no tears. I briefly returned from boarding school to 'look after' my mother in her grief and attend the funeral. But I was dry-eyed throughout. In retrospect, I think dad's war wound must have been a major factor in our unsatisfactory relationship. He couldn't engage in the kinds of activities that dads are meant to do with their sons. For example, although I was in my early 60s when my own son achieved adolescence, I was able to play outdoor games with him, such as cricket and tennis – in both of which he soon trounced me. Looking back, I suspect my dad never wanted children. Having risked his life at such a young age and narrowly surviving, I guess he decided his path in life was simply to write, an ambition he pursued to his dying day. Physical procreation was of no interest to him: his books were his babies.

As a man, if one doesn't actively want children, it's very difficult to be a good father, as I myself know all too well.

Spike Milligan, the comedian who was also a deep depressive, was asked what he felt was his most important role in life (Milligan, 2023). He answered, 'being a good father'. He was indeed a good father (as he said somewhat wryly, with the help of a housekeeper) for 7 lone years, as his adult children testify, but then he left them for 6 months to have an extended honeymoon with his second wife: would he ever return? They wondered. He did. So, for him, 'being a good father' was a role that clashed with loyalty to his wife. When he had been a single parent, he had tiptoed through the garden, and they had followed him, as he exhorted them to whisper – what were they following? The child inside himself, which helped him to devise such exciting games, got firmly turned off when he went on honeymoon. We have no record of his feelings about this.

References

Alvarez, Anne (1992) *Live Company*, Routledge
Alvarez, Anne (2012) *The Thinking Heart*, Routledge
Freud, S. (1923). The ego and the id. In J. Strachey (Ed. & Trans.), *The standard edition of the complete psychological works of Sigmund Freud* (Vol. 19). Hogarth Press.
Horne, A., & Lanyado, M. (eds). (2005). *An independent mind*. Routledge.
Jefferies, R. (1883). *The story of my heart: My autobiography*. Longmans, Green & Co.
Mantel, H. (2005). *The mirror and the light*. Fourth Estate.
Milligan, S. (2023). *Love, light and peace*, BBC TV4, 7 January.
Wroe, A. (2016). *Six facets of light*. Random House UK.

3 Fathers and Sons

This poem by Lewis Carroll expresses the contempt a young man may experience, at a conscious or unconscious level, for his father:

> "You are old, Father William," the young man said,
> "And your hair has become very white;
> And yet you incessantly stand on your head—
> Do you think, at your age, it is right?"
> "In my youth," Father William replied to his son,
> "I feared it might injure the brain;
> But now that I'm perfectly sure I have none, [*That's what his son thinks – JE*]
> Why, I do it again and again."
> "You are old," said the youth, "as I mentioned before,
> And have grown most uncommonly fat;
> Yet you turned a back-somersault in at the door—
> Pray, what is the reason of that?"

The poem first appeared in Carroll's (1865) book, *Alice's Adventures in Wonderland*, recited by Alice herself in the chapter entitled, 'Advice from a Caterpillar'. Father William then tries to sell the young man some healing ointment. He declares he kept his jaw strong by arguing legal cases with his wife. Then he threatens to kick the young man downstairs. The poem poked fun at current societal expectations around ageing and physical appearance, and I'd also like to suggest that Lewis Carroll might have been poking fun, at an unconscious level, at his own ageing father Charles Dodgson, who was an Anglican cleric, scholar and author, and the Archdeacon of Richmond. He had four sons, including Lewis, who was the oldest boy, and seven daughters, all home-educated. In the one extant photograph, Lewis' father looks like a stern and uncompromising figure, who 'did his best to instil' High Church Anglo-Catholic views into his children. So Carroll, reading *Pilgrim's Progress* when he was 7 years old, came from a family of High Church Anglicans, and was 'afflicted' by a stammer. This stammer may have been the result of trying and failing to attach to an authoritarian father (Klaniczay, 2000).

It was Carl Jung who coined the term 'father complex' to add gravity to the weight of his debt (and final split) from Freud. The father complex also stood at the conceptual core of Freud's *Totem and Taboo* (1912–1913). Even after the break with Jung, the father complex remained important in Freud's theorising in the 1920s – for example, it appeared prominently in *The Future of an Illusion* (Freud, 1927). Others in Freud's circle wrote freely of the complex's ambivalent nature. However, by 1946, and Otto Fenichel's detailed summary of the first psychoanalytic half-century, the father complex tended to be subsumed under the broader scope of the Oedipus complex as a whole (as has been indicated here).

After the Freud/Jung split, Jung equally continued to use the father complex to illuminate father-son relations, when Jung noted how a positive father complex could produce an over-readiness to believe in authority. Freud and Jung had both used the father complex as a tool to illuminate their own personal relationship. For example, as their early intimacy deepened, Jung had written to Freud asking him to 'let me enjoy your friendship not as that of equals but as that of father and son'. In retrospect, however, both Jungians and Freudians would note how Jung was impelled to question Freud's theories in a way that pointed to the existence of a negative father complex beneath the positive one – beneath his chosen and overt stance of being the favourite son. It is perhaps no surprise that the complex ultimately led to and fuelled conflicts between the pair, with Jung accusing Freud of 'treating your pupils like patients ... Meanwhile you are sitting pretty on top, as father'. In his attempts to struggle free from his psychoanalytic father figure, Jung would reject the term 'father complex' as Viennese name-calling – despite his own use of it in the past to illuminate precisely such situations. Jung's own birth father, Paul, was the youngest son of a professor of medicine, but his own hopes of achieving wealth came to nothing, and he didn't progress beyond the status of being an impoverished rural pastor of the Swiss Reformed Church. So, for Jung, as a role model, he had not been hugely significant, even though Jung described Freud as 'sitting pretty on top, as father'. The idea of the father complex had originally evolved to deal with the heavy Victorian patriarch; by the new millennium, however, there had developed instead a postmodern preoccupation with the *loss* of paternal authority – the absence of the father. But is he ever really absent or lost? Alongside the shift from a Freudian emphasis on the role of the father to object relation's theory stress on the mother (from Freud as father to Klein as mother, you might suggest), what psychoanalysis tended to single out was the search for the father, and the negative effects of the switched-off father. It has even been suggested from a French perspective that the expression is almost completely absent from contemporary psychoanalysis. Although post-Lacanians continue to debate the idea, a postmodern dictionary of psychoanalysis is nonetheless more likely to have an entry instead for James M. Herzog's (1980) term 'Father hunger': the son's longing for and need of contact with a father figure. However, Jungians such as Erich Neumann (1954) continued to use the concept of the father complex to explore the father-son relationship and its implications for issues of authority, noting, on the one hand, how a premature identification with the father, foreclosing the generational struggle, could lead to a thoughtless conservatism, whereas, on the other hand, the perennial rebel against the father complex is found in the archetype of the eternal adolescent son. Eating disorders writer Margo D. Maine used the concept of 'father hunger' in her book, *Fathers, Daughters and Food* (Maine, 1991), with particular emphasis on the relationship with the daughter (see Chapter 4 in this volume, Fathers and Daughters). Such father hunger, prompted by paternal absence, may leave the daughter with an unhealthy kind of narcissism, and with a prevalent search for external sources of self-esteem. Maine further examined the longing that all children have for connection with fathers, and how an unmet hunger for a father influences disordered eating and other mental illnesses. In contemporary psychoanalytic theory, James M. Herzog's (1980) *Father Hunger: Explorations with Adults and Children* addresses the unconscious longing experienced by many males and females for an involved father. Also, the importance of fatherly provisions for both sons and daughters during their respective developmental stages is examined in the writings of Michael J. Diamond (2007). Jungians have emphasised the power of *parent hunger*, forcing one repeatedly to seek out unrealised parts of the father archetype in the outside world. One answer for men is to move into having their own children to find the lost father within themselves, the internal father, and hand him on to their children, thereby shifting from demanding parental guidance themselves to providing it to their offspring. The notion of the 'father complex' still holds sway in culture at large. For example, the poet and philosopher Czeslaw Milosz (2004) wrote of Albert Einstein, 'everything about him appealed to my father complex, my yearning for a protector and leader'. Bob Dylan's choice of pseudonym has been linked to the father complex, as a rejection of his actual father and his paternal name of Zimmerman. After that choice, however, he would seek out a series of father figures, or 'idols' as he called them, to act as father confessor, before leaving each one behind again in turn. However, English novelist D. H. Lawrence dismissed the idea of the father complex as applied to himself, calling it a fool's complex. So, there you have it: as Bob Dylan so famously said, 'the answers are blowing in the wind'.

Which raises the question, 'Will I be to my son as my father was to me?' The article by Tracey et al. (1996) is the narrative of a first-time father with a son born 7 weeks early by caesarean section. Alongside the anxiety and trauma of his infant's birth and his wife's illness following the unexpected and traumatic caesarean delivery, another inner and much darker drama is being relived. The father, Michael, shows all the wounds of a battered child. He asks two vital questions: Will I be to my son as my father was to me? Will my son be to me as I was to my father? Fearful and at first unvoiced questions, where the developing interviews gave them a voice over time. The authors respected Michael's sharing of the early and fearful days and nights when his infant first came home. They sometimes found it hard to empathise with his running away to hide in work, until they understood what he was hiding from. Most poignant was his struggle with his anger and hurt with his father, and his desire to understand, 'Why?', so that he would not be like that to his own son. A sensitive revelation of life being born inside him anew, as he made contact with his real infant as well as his psychic infant within. This was a striking example of the therapeutic use of the research interview space, and the interviewer as a containing object.

Sigmund Freud was dubbed 'the Father of Psychoanalysis', and he too had a biological father as well as those on whose ideas he built. His father Jakob Freud was an averagely successful wool merchant, and at 40, he had two grown-up sons when he got married for the third time to Amalie Nathanson. 'Sigi' was the first and the favourite of her children. Amalie felt he was destined to be a great man, as indeed he did become. Amalie had seven other children, and some of them ended up in Hitler's gas chambers. Sigi was outraged by his father's lack of heroism when his father told him the story of having his cap knocked off: 'Jew, get off the pavement.' His father just picked up his cap and walked on. So, we start with a father whom 'Sigi' definitely did not consider to be a role model. His father's 'feet of clay' were sadly evident to his son. Sigi had downplayed the threat of Nazism, had to be strongly persuaded to relocate to London, with his daughter Anna (did she have her own issues with her father's feet of clay?), and four of his sisters, in their eighties, were trapped. Marie and Paulina went to Treblinka, Rosa to Auschwitz and Adolfine to Theresienstadt. As Clive James (2008, p. 228) said, 'The real psychodrama was too big for him to see. He could have escaped sooner, and from exile he could have saved all his relatives. He never grasped that Nazi destructiveness was a complete mind in itself.' His theories have seeped into so much of our modern media, and writers may both consciously and unconsciously use his ideas, as his legacy continues to be debated.

Now we go on with a modern father who was adopted, and who then reflected on his adopted father's difficult start in life when reflecting on his own, though he did not, at least in this account, entertain fantasies about his own birth parents. (*It is possible that these were too deeply hidden in his mind for him to access them – JE*)

> I was born on January 5, 1947, in the House of Redeeming Love; an orphanage in Oklahoma City, Oklahoma, USA. Two weeks later, my new parents adopted me and took me to their home along with their daughter, who was also adopted, my sister Lee. My adoptive father was a career military officer, Air Force. My childhood memories of my family were all in the context of his military career. When I was six years old, my Dad was appointed to a NATO assignment, a Classified Document Center near Naples, Italy. We moved there as a family. Our four years there were the most shaping of my childhood. My stay-at-home mother was the parent who connected with me personally. My father was the provider. He was a steady presence, engaged with our family as a

whole, but not as much with me individually. One Christmas I received a much desired HO Marklin (high-quality German) train. It remains my favourite Christmas present of my life. My father made frequent military trips to a NATO office in Germany. In connection with the train set, he would buy me a present, a new HO train car on each trip, exactly what I wanted. As an adolescent, I was increasingly differentiating from my family. In high school, my life was filled with activities: student governance, choir, drama and sports. My parents lived a quiet life at home. At times, my father's efforts to help me or connect with me, were along the lines of encouraging me (or requiring me) to settle down. About that time, my father was given another overseas assignment for a year and a half, this time without family. He returned as I was nearing the end of my high school years. Somehow I knew that it was good for me that he was gone. When he returned, my activity path was set. Our relationship continued without disruption, or conflict. It was even warm, at times, but I was finding my own way. While I was still living at home, my father retired from the military. He and my mother began to travel a great deal. I started dating Stephne (no 'a', no 'i') soon after entering college. She and I became engaged to be married (*they are now celebrating their 55th anniversary – JE*). I transferred to a college in Seattle. It was the late 1960s; I became involved in anti-war efforts. Departing from my family's' more conservative political perspective, I was drawn to the emerging counter-culture, with convictions about compassion and justice. In less than 2 years, Stephne and I had our first child. Later, I participated in an anti-war protest in Washington, DC, and was arrested and went to jail, spending the night with Rabbi Abraham Heschel and Benjamin Spock. I entered a graduate school and attended seminary. I joined the Farm Worker movement with Caesar Chavez, working for justice for farm workers. All of this was the journey of finding my own path. My peace and justice involvements were in sharp contrast to my father's conservative military patriotic values. Never did I have an argument or debate with my father about these values. It was not my father's way to have arguments. I was finding a different path from my father (and mother). Upon reflection, I now know that being adopted was a subtle but deep aspect of this differentiation. (*This is the only time that the fantasy of birth parents might have obtruded – JE*) It was not until my thirties that I began to desire a more meaningful connection with my parents. I had settled into a vocation as a Presbyterian minister. I had returned to graduate school and earned a doctorate. I had found a path where seeking justice and living the Christian faith conjoined. My identity and vocation had become stable. I was serving large congregations. While my father and I sharply differed on political views, we continued to share a common faith conviction. My father was genuinely proud of me and my vocation. As the parents grew older, they decided to move back from the east coast USA to California, moving into the neighborhood where we lived and I worked. We welcomed their connection. I was serving a large and prominent congregation. They became active members in the church, finding a place with special recognition as my parents. I was pleased to have them nearby and had regular contact. After a number of years went by, I changed ministry locations and moved to Spokane, Washington, some 1,300 miles north of San Diego to serve a congregation there. My mother passed away soon after. With her passing, my father moved in to our home and lived with us for a year and a half. As he was aging, his activities were more restricted, though he enjoyed attending the worship at the church where I was the minister. He volunteered in the church's Alzheimer's support team, and a senior fellowship group. He then remarried at age 90. I performed the ceremony. And he moved into his new wife's home. Our relationship was warm and friendly. He lived to be 100. I don't remember my father having any explicit ambitions for me. Only that I attend and graduate from college. (*Again, no mention of the fantasy about birth parents – JE*) Because my father's temperament and ideas were so different than mine, I am glad that he didn't try to influence my career focus. Because I had been very good at maths and science in high school and because my adoptive grandfather was a chemical engineer, I started my first year in college as an engineering major. In a matter of weeks I realised that was a poor choice for me. In hindsight I can see that it would have been a terrible, terrible choice. Wrong temperament. I became a business/advertising/public relations major for some time. That was much better. Later, I changed again and became an education major. That was still better. After college, I attended a graduate school of theology, which led to a degree in theology and a vocation as a minister. That was an excellent fit for me. My relationship with my father was mixed and interwoven. On the one hand, we were fated to be fundamentally different in temperament and interests. Even more deeply, there was an underlying difference created by the consequence of adoption itself. Yet, he, with my mother, provided a very stable and warm home. Our family life seemed to be without tension. I was loved and supported. My father did the best he knew how to be a parent to an adopted child so very different than himself. My father's father had abandoned his family when my Dad was a young boy. He grew up without a father. My Dad had a younger brother. His mother had only a few years of education. My Dad took on responsibilities for family income, dropping out of school at about age 12, working in a grocery store. Through the support of an uncle, he was able to return to school, eventually graduating from college – earning a degree in chemistry and languages. He had not gained any fathering experience as a child. Thus, in contrast to his own father, he went on to provide a very stable home. When my parents adopted me, they soon found me to be a nervous baby. As a child, I had trouble settling down and faced difficulty in concentrating on school work. I don't think my adopted father knew what to make of me, or how to relate to me. By contrast, my adopted mother was highly engaged in my life. My difficulty in settling down and doing school work only made her more involved. She was not overbearing, but she was in truth overinvolved. I think Dad simply left it to her to relate to me. I have heard that adopted children are at times less secure in pushing against their parents as they find their own path. I think I had a version of that. Ironically, even though he was always supportive, because my father was not greatly involved, it made it easier to find a life and a path that was not like his.

Eventually, my most basic view of my father and my parents becomes one of gratitude. And it is genuine gratitude that remains. I experience it to this day. I became a father myself a few days after I graduated from college. Stephne and I married after our junior year, and a year and a half later, we became parents, one day before I turned 23. I was unexpectedly overwhelmed by the wonder of the experience. It was six and a half years until we had our second son, Matthew. The parental love I had been given with Steve's birth now extended to embrace another child. That's the way love is. It can always expand and grow without diminishing the previous loves. (*But this is not always how firstborns experience it, when they for the first time have to share parental love, as many other accounts show. They feel they have been rejected and ejected from their place as 'King Baby' – JE*) It was always important to me to be a good father to my two sons. While my own father had done the best he could to provide a stable and caring home for me, I wanted to do more for my own sons (*who, of course, were not adopted*). I liked kids. In their childhood, I enjoyed playing with them; building with toy blocks, playing out of doors. I particularly enjoyed reading to them at bedtime – especially *The Chronicles of Narnia*. As they grew, I wanted to share with them activities that I had come to enjoy, particularly water skiing and snow skiing. Teaching them myself to snow ski was another highlight. I just loved the experience. Having their little bodies snuggled up against mine as we rode chairlifts and introducing them to the adventure of skiing was delightful beyond words. As they passed through childhood into adolescence, I sought to adjust. Along with Stephne, we saw them achieving more independence. Steve and Matthew were both easy to raise. Neither of them was difficult, rebellious or troublesome. Both of them had positive educational experiences through high school. We were living in San Diego when Steve went away to college. I remember watching him drive away in a little Honda station wagon. I went upstairs to his bedroom, fell on his bed, and sobbed like a baby. When Matthew went to college, we drove him to the campus and left him there checking into his dorm room. Again, the sadness ran very deep.

Steve and his wife are now themselves 'empty nesters' too. Their children have left 'the nest' and ventured into the wider world.

I was more involved with my two sons than my father was with me. I played with them as children, building with blocks, showing affection, reading to them at bedtime. In the back of my mind, I saw this as being intentionally more connected than my father had been with me. I enjoyed them. I attended as many of their sporting events, choir concerts, school plays as I could. I loved talking with them about all sorts of things: books, current events, church life and their aspirations. However, my ministerial vocation required heavy time involvement. I don't think I realised it at the time, but because we rarely had weekends like an average family, as I had so many nights out at church meetings, our time together as a family was far less than many families had. I was always highly focused on being effective at my vocation. In hindsight, I could have been more intentional about compensating for the demands of ministry and cost to our family life, with some creativity and effort. I wish I had done so. We are very, very fortunate that we did not have a divided family. Our sons' families are intact. We have lived in close proximity to our sons, their wives, and our grandchildren. This is a rare thing in the western world today. On a couple of rare occasions, we have had some episodes of anger with one of our sons and spouse. However, that has passed long ago.

While I was more involved and closer to my sons than my father was to me, both of our sons are even more connected to their children than I was to mine.

Some of that is the result of their vocations being so different than mine was. Some of it is that parents today cling more closely to their children. Parents today are more fearful and more protective than we were. To a certain degree, that is very understandable. I feel that as a family, we are very fortunate, and as a father, I am fortunate to have relatively positive relationships with our sons and their families.

Fortunate, indeed. This is a father who has passed on good memories and good feelings and thinks that his sons too have received what he gave and amplified it.

Below are the memories of someone who became a priest, did not marry or have children:

Dad was a constant figure in my life until he died, and he has remained pivotal. It was not that we were emotionally close, but more that he was always 'there'. He was interpreted to me by my mother. In many ways, she interpreted him to himself. She was the 'stronger' partner. He was more biddable and was happy to follow a stronger personality. He was dutiful and a 'provider' of the 'handing over the pay packet' kind (he worked his way up in the building trade, working all his life for Sir Robert McAlpine). He has a special place for me, and for all his children, because of his sayings: these were/are like scripture for us: 'You would think there wasn't a pot of paint in the land' as we drove home through a dreary Scottish town. 'I want to congratulate you for driving all the way from North Berwick to Tranent with the choke out', as my brother preened himself after a driving lesson. 'You just stuck the screwdriver in and buggered off', after finding one of his beloved tools finger-deep in the garden. 'No dirty stuff' if the conversation got a bit blue. 'Look at the boy with the piercing eyes' about the Italian football referee Perluigi Collina. 'More, more' when putting sugar in his tea ... 'Teeth like a duck's foot' on unbrushed teeth. 'Give me one of those cork-tips' having forgotten his Player's Navy Cut (un-tipped). 'Three bars of the (electric) fire on and the television all snow' when giving out in the morning about the irresponsible late-night drinking of his children. All of these were his uniqueness. In this he wasn't following anyone else's lead. The car was his domain. He tinkered with, and 'fixed', it. He was the only driver in the family and for years was an example of the way to do it. It was only after some years of driving ourselves that we realised that he had no special driving powers. His greatest purchase was a red Volvo 122. My brother and I were so proud of him (and my Mam too?) when he drove up the drive of our boarding school (summer picnic) in this very classy motor. The forgetfulness of Alzheimer's cushioned the experience of us selling his car when he was in his eighties. I don't know the origins of his love of time pieces. But he collected them and stored them in his little workshop. The 'tick-tocking' was a feature of any search there for glue or hedge-clippers or overalls. He never failed to comment on a new watch sported by any of us. Occasionally, he would say something that let you know that he was aware that he wasn't functioning properly, as Alzheimer's increased. On one occasion we sat next to each other for tea, and he asked me, 'Is that a new watch?' I replied that it was newish but that I had had it for several months. Again, he asked me, 'Is that is a new watch'? And again, 'Is that a new watch?' After perhaps the fifth exchange, I pulled down the hem of my shirt cuff to cover the watch. He spotted this and said, 'There is no point in covering it up' – almost like a gentle reprimand for trying to ward off his questioning. My mother was the dominant 'aspirant' for her child. Top of her list of aspirations for me was to become a priest. They both had a strong Catholic cultural background. As in most things, my father was more acquiescent. My main concern was to make sure I wasn't following my Mam's vocation but my own!

Extract from my Journal of Dad's Death

Thursday, 8 May 2014 (Rome)

14.00 The first inkling came when there was an odd phone call from Lawrence, my brother-in-law. When I answered, there was that strange noise of an unintentional call. That is what I presumed it was. Some minutes later, I spotted a text from Mary, 'Dad has taken a turn for the worse, Mam has gone over (to the hospital), we should make arrangements to go.' I made a conscious decision to go to supervision and see how things were when I got back. It was just as I went in to supervision that I got Mary's message letting me know that Dad had died. The supervision was a gift. I thought I could man it out, but I was a little emotional at the beginning. The supervisor was very present and empathetic. It gave me a chance to work through my initial emotions. Things moved quite quickly when I got back to college. Tears welled up in the principal's eyes when I told him. After which I got on with contacting family, cancelling appointments and making travelling arrangements … I put a notice on the board: the team were caring and thoughtful, allowing me to head off early.

Friday, 9 May 2014 (Rome/Donegal)

I was in for Morning Prayer and breakfast, making one or two final arrangements, and being comforted by people. Peter took me to Ciampino. The rest of the journey was zoned out. Mary and Lawrence were already there when I arrived, as were Gerry and Lindsay. Jim arrived shortly afterwards. There was a short service at the hospital where Dad had been in repose since the morning before. Leo, Fabes and Laurence had arrived by this time. We said the prayers of the Church, along with a decade of the rosary, and then took him back to St Joseph's Avenue. We said more prayers and another decade of the rosary as neighbours and friends gathered round. The coffin was open on both occasions and remained open throughout the next 36 hours. We reconvened at 22.00 for the rosary in full, the Glorious Mysteries. I led the 1st and 4th, Mam led the 2nd, Mary the 3r and Pat the 5th. People sat chatting for a while, before going to bed.

Saturday, 10 May 2014 (Donegal)

Lawrence and I were up first, and out for the papers and early fresh air. The young generation arrived promptly, having been on a 07.00 flight to Derry, had breakfast, and when Eamonn and Susan arrived, we all went out to the lovely house that they had hired for the following three days. I saw Fr Peoples and had a few winning bets in town before a Chinese supper for the home crowd. Eamonn was billeted with me. Rosary again at 22.00 with Eamonn choking up on his 4th decade. Bed was a bit later tonight.

Sunday, 11 May 2014 (Donegal)

Lawrence and I up sharpish for papers and shopping. There was a general melee until 12.20 when the undertakers came, we had some brief prayers, and the four boys plus John and Paul shouldered the coffin to the hearse and thence to The Four Masters. Frs Peoples and McLoon joined us for the funeral. It was on Good Shepherd Sunday, and that provided an easy image to bid the old man farewell. The Browns had come down, as had Michael and Bernadette Breen, along with Leonard, Martin and Eamonn, Josie's boys. The grave is in Clar Chapel Cemetery, in the top right-hand corner. Great spot. Dad is buried next to Paul Cox, who has shadowed our lives throughout. It was amazing that they should die within a week of each other – 2 and 8 May, respectively. Lunch at Dom's was a big success and, indeed, a group of Achilles' warriors would stay drinking until 23.00, when Lindsay and I acted as a taxi service to take them to their various welcome beds. Mary was a stalwart throughout, and did remarkably well.

Monday, 12 May 2014 (Donegal)

Sore heads for many this morning, with staggered (!) departures throughout the day. Lawrence and I went up to Stranorlar to formally register the death and receive the death certificate. Mammy, Mary, Lawrence and I had mince patties and chips for supper. I had tied up a lot of loose ends before that, printing off boarding passes, returning stoles and 'paying the priest', visiting Pat, returning the wheelchair and buying the mince. We watched 'Prey' and went to bed early. I said my farewells, because I was off early the next day. I had found an old clock of Dad's, which would fittingly wake me in time. Tick-tock ... he still ticks away in my mind, more as I grow older myself. (*Is that a new watch? That became a fixure inside this man's mind ... – JE*)

And who holds whose hand? The award-winning poet Richar Meier has generously given me this (unpublished) poem, quoted in full here:

So this is where it comes from
Two or three hours before my father dies.
Sometimes he puts his hands up in the air,
sometimes it's like he's searching for a piece
of non-existent string or thread.
And once or twice he reaches for my hand.

When I hold or used to hold
my children's hands, I'd notice
the way my thumb, the pad of it,
would automatically, in a circling motion, rub
their fingers, in a soothing, I'm-here sort of way.

And now my father, even now,
begins to rub my fingers with his thumb,
so even though it's me who's holding his hand,
my father is my father to the end,
and really it is he who's holding mine.

References

Carroll, L. (1865). *Alice's adventures in Wonderland*. Macmillan.
Diamond, M. J. (2007). *My Father Before Me*. W. W. Norton & Company.
Freud, S. (1912–1913). *Totem and taboo*. Hogarth Press.
Freud, S. (1927). *The future of an illusion*. Hogarth Press.
Herzog, J. M. (1980). *Father hunger: Explorations with adults and children*. The Analytic Press.
James, C. (2008). *Cultural amnesia: Notes in the margin of my time*. Picador.
Klaniczay, S. (2000). On childhood stuttering and the theory of clinging. *Journal of Child Psychotherapy*, 26(1), 97–115.
Maine, M. D. (1991). *Fathers, daughters and food*. Gurze Designs & Books.
Milosz, C. (2004). The fate of the religious imagination. *New Perspectives Quarterly*, 21(4).
Neumann, E. (1954). *The origins and history of consciousness*. Princeton University Press.
Tracey, N., Blake, P., Warren, B., Hardy, H., Enfield, S., & Shein, P. (1996). Will I be to my son as my father was to me? Narrative of a father with a premature baby. *Journal of Child Psychotherapy*, 22(2), 168–194.

4 Fathers and Daughters

The Subjection of Women is an essay by English philosopher, political economist and civil servant John Stuart Mill, published in 1869, with ideas he developed jointly with his wife Harriet Taylor Mill. He submitted the finished manuscript of their collaborative work *On Liberty* (1859) soon after her untimely death in late 1858, and then continued work on *The Subjection of Women* until its completion in 1861 (Longmans Green).

At the time of its publication, the essay's argument for equality between the sexes was an affront to European conventional norms regarding the status of men and women. The essay is regarded as one of the most fundamental texts underlying the formation of modern-day feminism, influencing authors such as Betty Friedan, who was in-part responsible for 'second-wave' feminism in the 1960s.

Mill was an acclaimed liberal philosopher, publicist, politician and scientist who championed the march for an egalitarian society. He is more commonly known for writing the text 'On Liberty' in which he called for central principles in order to build a liberal democratic society during the Enlightenment in Europe. 'On Liberty' was crucial in identifying the balance between authority of the government and individuality of the citizen; these two themes are significant in *The Subjection of Women* (1861) as Mill argues for a less authoritarian government to allow for more individuality of women, which would subsequently enhance happiness for higher numbers of people … that is, the other half of the human race.

Mill's overarching thesis, based on a combination of liberal and utilitarian assumptions, is that the inequality of men and women is unjust as well as harmful, both for individuals and for the progression of society. This has been similarly stated by Elizabeth Day who says that, 'Mill argues that more people existing alongside one another on an equal footing means increased competition, with an advantageous effect on human moral and intellectual development, both individual and social.' Although Mill's beliefs were heavily influenced by Mary Wollstonecraft and Harriet Taylor Mill, we can see him as revolutionary, as he was the first male to advocate feminism in a time when feminism in the political discourse was discouraged.

DOI: 10.4324/9781003521846-5

Modern critics, such as Jennifer Ball and Moira Gatens, argue that Mill tends to focus on the sociolegal aspects of the subordination of women and not on the cultural aspects of the issue. He argues that 'the principle which regulates the existing social relations between the two sexes—the legal subordination of one sex to the other—is wrong in itself, and now one of the chief hindrances to human improvement; and that it ought to be replaced by a principle of perfect equality, admitting no power or privilege on the one side, nor disability on the other' (Mill, 1869).

Mill here bases the inequality of men and women on the legal aspects of society. He says that the law confines women to take on domestic roles, being excluded from decision-making parts of society, such as politics and business. Mill understands that the central reason for this oppression comes from the male's physical strength. Men are physically bigger than women, and it was common to think at the time that a man's brain was larger than that of a wwomen. Mill had debunked the myth that women's grains are generally smaller than men's, saying that 'any of the mental differences supposed to exist between women and men are but the natural effect of the differences in their education and circumstances and indicate no radical difference, far less radical inferiority, of nature' (Mill, 1869). Mill assumes that the more influence reason has in society, the less importance physical strength will have – 'in this state, women will no longer be disadvantaged, as physical strength becomes less important as civilisation advances' (Szapuová, 2006).

By stating that the subordination of women is one of the 'chief hindrances to human improvement', Mill is indicating that the oppression of women poses negative consequences on the lives of women, but of men as well – hence preventing the progression of society as a whole. Mill argues that for society to progress, women must be able to be treated as equals. This is because any inequality represents a barrier to the advancement of an entire society and is also an obstacle to progress on an individual level. Mill justifies the need of the emancipation of women to develop their personal talents so as to realise the maximum of their personal happiness, and as a result, contribute to the development of society. This argument is based on liberal principles of equal opportunities and individual free choice, but also utilitarian principles of the well-being of the maximum number of people. In this way, Mill transcended his own time: in the 1860s, there was no female suffrage, women could not own property (it was given to their husbands) and women did not have equal access to education. To think of a woman as an equal was only really acknowledged by most men half a century later, when finally, some women were allowed to vote.

By contrast, several contemporary feminists, such as Moira Gatens, have criticized this argument, suggesting that Mill is not in fact interested in the emancipation of women on its own, but rather the benefits that it would bring to society and, therefore, for men. Gatens stresses that Mill's central argument for the emancipation of women is based on the need of intellectual progress among men, which cannot occur unless women also progress. Therefore, Mill favours women's emancipation because the progress of the human race depends on it (Gatens, 1991). From this, many feminists take Mill's liberal feminism to be 'masculinist' and perhaps not so revolutionary. Read and choose.

What impact did Mill's work have on the law today?

Although we can't discount Mill's influence, his impact of lobbying politicians and changing the law was limited, but he did inspire many feminists, who would later change the law themselves. During Mill's time as a liberal MP, he supported the Married Women's Property Bill in 1868, in which he was critical of the idea that husbands, through their right to vote, served as their protectors of their wives. He declares in parliament:

> Now, by the common law of England, all that a wife has, belongs absolutely to the husband; he may tear it all from her, squander every penny of it in debauchery, leave her to support by her labour herself and her children, and if by heroic exertion and self-sacrifice she is able to put by something for their future wants, unless she is judicially separated from him he can pounce down upon her savings, and leave her penniless.
> (Deb, 1867)

In 1870, this hugely important Bill passed as the Married Woman's Property Act, which allowed women to own their own income and property in marriage. This was the first radical step toward the emancipation of women. Although he contributed to the passing of the bill, he was overshadowed by the work of Barbara Bodichon, a women's rights activist, who had a more central role of promoting women's rights. She contributed by writing several essays, one being 'Reasons for the Enfranchisement of Women' (Bodichon, 1866), and using political activism by creating small pressure groups, which would lobby the government. It also important to note that a majority of MPs is needed to pass a bill. Therefore, we can understand that a large number of MPs (who were all male) voted for this bill.

Mill had a role in passing this bill, but his role was limited to using political action. Some women were given the right to vote in 1918, which has been argued was speeded up by female involvement in society after World War I, and by feminist activists such as Emmeline Pankhurst, and not by Mill's work. Baby steps?

And so, Mill's essay on 'The Subjection of Women' perhaps influenced some men to change their view on women; however, it did not have enough substance to change the law.

Mill's ultimate solution for ending the oppression of women was not equal opportunity, but spousal friendship. Mill emphasized the need for the end of 'marital slavery' and for establishing a friendship within marriage.

Mill underlines that the intrinsic reason why women are degraded to slaves in marriage is systemic discrimination in society. He states that women are not free to marry and are not in any case free within marriage. This comes as a result of economic pressure to marry – women cannot acquire education or earn money in public life and must resort to marriage to have an income. This constrains women into a cyclical sphere of slavery within marriage, as women are forced to become dependent on men for basic needs. He goes on to say that since humans are equal, the fact that someone is born a woman shouldn't determine her position in society and customs should not 'ordain that to be born a girl instead of a boy, any more to be born black instead of white, or a commoner instead of a nobleman, shall decide the person's position through all life' (Mill, 1869). He based his feminist views on the harm principle – the idea that individuals should be free to do anything except harm other individuals. Female oppression is an example of harming individuality and prohibiting freedom. Although liberal views were not revolutionary at the time, no other liberal philosopher had yet outlined the fact that female oppression contradicts the liberal principles of individuality and freedom, perhaps because they didn't want females to advance in society. Is this another example, do we think, of male envy? Mill was the first liberal male to outline this and to understand the relationship that feminism and liberalism share. In this way, we can say Mill is a revolutionary.

Some feminists have denounced Mill's arguments on marriage saying they don't go far enough. Although Mill condemns the injustice of marital slavery, he assumes that equality before the law will eliminate the oppression of women and guarantee their equality, even if traditional gender roles remain in place. Mmmm ... It is the failure of Mill to address the problem of traditional gender roles that has caused some feminists to question Mill's work. Mill does not attack the traditional assumptions regarding the different responsibilities that men and women have in the household and accepts that when women marry, they should be responsible for taking care of the home and children while men provide income. Mill's naivety proves problematic, as he believes even the most liberated woman would continue to choose family over other activities. This has led many to believe that Mill should not be labelled as a revolutionary, as his beliefs are still old-fashioned.

But perhaps men hold greater respect for women now and see them as human beings with equal worth rather than domestic animals, enslaved by marriage.

To what extent was this change as a result of Mill? One could argue quite significantly that Mill laid out the principles of a reformed relationship in marriage. He described the perfect utopia in marriage, where two equal friends come together in cohabitation (as the Quakers have enshrined in their marriage vows, two friends coming together). Property was fundamental to liberal belief – 'life, liberty and property' were the three principles of liberalism – and now women were on path to achieve liberty. Mill also redefined the way men should think about their partners, revolutionising marriage, as it were. His essay on 'The Subjection of Women' came as a surprise to many, but ultimately changed the way men behaved towards women. As women became more equal in marriage, views on women in society slowly started to change.

Mill is regarded as one of the most interesting liberal feminists, and he revolutionised the discourse among men about women. Society had advanced a long way (and will go on advancing) since Aristotle gave his description of the female as a deformed male (Freud with his notion of penis envy continued this trope). Mill's feminist philosophy brought about change in society unlike any other male who proceeded him – so, he can be seen as a revolutionary.

Let's carry on this chapter with a story that seems sad now but was considered to be the norm before there were any other avenues to go down, despite the publication of John Stuart Mills' tract, *The Subjection of Women* in 1869. Old habits die hard, as this account from the 1950s shows us:

> From my point of view when I was very young I remember thinking my dad preferred my brother to me. We were born 20 months apart, so I don't remember a time before my brother wasn't there, but Dad seemed to enjoy doing things with him more. (*Here we have fathers identifying with sons, so sons then identity with fathers, and the not so merry go round goes on. This is the daughter's narrative – JE*)
>
> In the early 1950s, parent roles were more defined by male or female activities, so Dad made my brother fort, a crystal set a go-cart and offered various modelling sets. He seemed to spend much more time with him doing stuff. I don't think I was jealous, I just didn't expect anything different. (*at that time, feminine 'jealousy' was repressed, and disapproved of*)
>
> My job was to help Mum as much as I could. I remember my job at home at around 5–6 years old was to scrub the floor (*domestic slavery writ large – JE*) though I can't remember if my brother had a job. I taught myself to read before I went to school and loved drawing. My Dad loved making and mending things, woodwork and things that might be useful. Nothing was thrown away in case it came in handy, a trait I seem to have inherited. Mum was disabled with multiple sclerosis, and I remember my Dad cycled to work in the city during the week and did the washing and cooking at weekends, as Mum couldn't stand for a long time. There were no electrical aids back then, like slow cookers, automatic washing machines and microwaves, so sheets and towels were done in a boiler, and cooking was always on or in the gas stove.
>
> We also had my Mum's elderly great-uncle living with us for a time. He had dementia and became doubly incontinent, which meant Dad had a lot more work at home to contend with, and at quite a young age. He would have been in his mid thirties. I felt then, that Dad was always quite an angry person and had a quick temper, but now I wonder if deep

down he ever resented the restrictions placed on his life sometimes (*again, such feelings were disavowed and repressed*). First the war, then a family and looking after us all. He adored my Mum but looking back, they had no quality time on their own together. They decided that they would have children as soon as possible, as they knew Mum's disability would eventually become worse. As my brother and I grew up, Dad and I butted heads a lot. He was the authority figure in our house and made all the decisions. It seemed that because my brother was academically clever, Dad thought he would and should go far (which he did), and my life would be to get married and have children, full stop. (I eventually did my exams in my 30s partly to prove I had a brain too). He offered my brother driving lessons and apparently, I wasn't interested, although I don't remember that. I was a pretty sulky teenager, and Dad couldn't understand how much I wanted the same freedom my friends seemed to have. By now it was the start of the 1960s and I was developing as a young woman, but I always felt Dad would still have liked me to be his little girl, doing as I was told and wearing what he called 'suitable' clothes and shoes. I wanted to wear heels and fashionable clothes, but Dad thought fashion was stupid and felt I should look 'smart' at all times, even making me wear my grammar school blazer on holiday. I eventually joined a youth club, which gave me the freedom to meet other teenagers and relax away from Dad's strict eye. I recall asking if I could go to an all-night party at the youth club leader's house when I was 16, the relief when Dad said yes, and Dad baking a tin full of rock cakes for me to take in case my friends and I got hungry. It was sweet of him, but not really what teenagers in those days did. My brother left home to travel across America and Europe and do his own thing when he was a young man. Mum and Dad didn't seem unduly worried about him, but I know Dad would have kicked up a massive fuss if I had expressed a desire to do that. I got engaged and followed the role that was expected of me, married at 20 and had my two babies at 22 and 24. I was traumatised by my first daughter's birth, as the hospital insisted that you didn't pick your baby up unless it needed a feed or nappy change and cuddling was 'indulging' your baby (*Truby King's edicts were 'the norm' – JE*). It was a very ascetic experience, but being new to motherhood, I thought it must be right. A spell of post-natal depression followed with some very dark thoughts (*an unsurprising and very sad outcome of feeling 'inferior' – JE*). Dad soon put paid to that. He became such a loving grandfather and adored my baby. He sang to her, showed her round his garden, pointing out flowers when she was a few months old and basically taught me how to be a Mum and have fun with her. When my second daughter came along, he again showed a loving tenderness and patience with them both, and they loved being with him. He liked nothing more than making them laugh and playing with them.

But now we would think differently about this account. Is anatomy destiny? Women's status, though becoming more considered, is still grossly unequal to that of a man, and not simply around the question of equal pay. The thing forbidden to girls, especially in the nineteenth century, was freedom of speech, leading to freedom of thought, and eventually freedom of action. '...the "castration" of the girl in her childhood and adolescence does in fact take place via the lack of serious consideration that is afforded her' (Baker Miller, 1973, p. 311). It is the fate of girls not to be taken seriously by their parents. This may be one of the reasons for girls' gender dysphoria. This book gives an overview of psychoanalytic work about women since Karen Horney, who died in the middle of the twentieth century. Freud's psychoanalytic views of female development emphasised the importance of penis envy and the Oedipus complex. Resolution of the Oedipus complex resulted in what he called a 'neurotic' solution, a 'masculinity complex' or a normal feminine attitude involving acceptance of anatomic inferiority, passivity, masochism and narcissism. Modern psychoanalytic views have (*fortunately, we may say* – JE) rejected or reformulated many of these theories. Penis envy (and also vagina envy in men) is seen as a normal phase of development. Women have been found to develop strong, albeit different, superego structures. The female character triad has been questioned and the role of environmental factors emphasised. Efforts continue to develop a comprehensive well-integrated view of female psychology. Julia Kristeva, French philosopher, has a different view.

For Kristeva, femininity and masculinity are not necessarily tied to biological issues. Kristeva rejects the idea that men and women are intrinsically different. Instead, she sees identity as something fluid and ever-changing. Some feminist theorists see these ideas as liberating, and of course, this has links, as I suggested above, with the notion of gender dysphoria.

Here is a happier memory of a father, who though absent, kept his daughter in mind:

> Despite being a more or less absent father physically, he was always attentive if he couldn't be present, sending (which I still have) hundreds of postcards from wherever he was, and relevant to my interest at the time, for example, horses when I was horse-mad, and always packed with small writing and lots of information ... quite unlike my mother who would write letters to me at boarding school, in very large writing, saying nothing, but filling the pages with only a few lines, and always ending 'In haste'.

> When I was studying Art and Architecture for A level, he was in Italy a lot, and I would receive a postcard almost every other day, of interesting and relevant architectural places and of paintings. Perhaps largely to do with the deprivations of boarding schools, he was always rather grubby, the privilege of being sent away at an early age to places with little comfort or hot water, possibly set this precedent. I blame the cold water.

He always had a good sense of humour and care for others, particularly more so after he became involved with Buddhism. He also had psychotherapy in his late 60s and 70s, once offering to contribute to my having the same, as he said he realised a lot of his behaviour might have adversely affected me, but I declined as I said I preferred to let the silt stay at the bottom of the bucket, as it were, as I felt if we started stirring, it might never sink back down again. I think perhaps, thanks to him, I have always found humour an important way to deal with life.

He never had a real job. He had a good voice and was a singer and was quite obsessed with his voice. According to our dear Nanny, he could be very difficult to live with, and could not be disturbed or interrupted when practising, and even when his mother died they had to wait until he'd finished to tell him. He had quite a selfish streak about what he wanted, which remained throughout his life.

But his voice was lovely, and he had concerts round the world, including a debut at the Wigmore Hall in London, but never quite became successful. I have a video made by a friend, with a recording of him singing a Handel piece, recorded in his late 20s, before I was born. It is very beautiful and I can hear him in his voice as I always knew it. Despite being distant in my life, partly because of his difficult marriage to my mother, he had a much happier second marriage and a second son, and I have always got on with my step-siblings who had the advantage of him as a proper and present father. I believe he loved his children equally. When my step-mother was dying, he went to stay with her and despite them both then having other attachments, I was touched to see the love and affection still there, as they sat beside each other holding hands and reminiscing.

For the last 50 years of his life, he lived alone in Lausanne, but had, perhaps the most important last love of his life, a woman from a simple background, who adored him, and he was surrounded by her children and grandchildren with care and affection, and the highlight of every week, was their large family get-together at the local pizzeria, where her grandchildren would climb onto his lap, to his delight, as he sat beaming, calling him 'Grandpere Eduoard', so he ended his days surrounded by love. Despite attempts from one family member to get him back to England to an old people's home, his lack of enthusiasm was summed up to me by his response to my asking how he felt about the idea, saying that it would break his heart to leave.

Antoinette, was his last and, to my mind, his strongest and most uncomplicated love. His eccentricities were legion and never failed to amaze and amuse me. For probably the last 15 years or so, he wore round his neck a label in French and English, stating that if he were to be found dead, he did not want to be buried for a week until it was definitely established that he was gone. He had a horror of a condition he'd heard of, where you can appear dead then come back to life in a coffin (shades of Edgar Allan Poe's *The Fall of the House of Usher*): the Lazarus effect, as I think it is also known). I have a marvellous photo of him sitting at the top of my stairs, in somewhat grubby long johns, pairs worn year round, and a cap with Corsica written on it with THE label around his neck. As it was, he was cremated, he died in Switzerland so I'm sure they established had gone.

He had wide and varied interests and was very knowledgeable and well read, and latterly took to writing letters to papers and authors on a wide variety of subjects. His interest and knowledge of Buddhism lasted to the end of his life, and he would visit ashrams in Lausanne and was friendly with many people there. This involvement made him very uncritical and compassionate of others, always looking for alternative reasons for their aggression or unhappiness, which was a good trait, but would occasionally annoy me if I wanted him to concur with my dislike of someone! So that was my Father, 'Pop', a mix of so much, as I said at the start, like us all perhaps, with so many shades of personality, but he had a good heart...

Lisa Maria Presley, daughter of Elvis, died of a heart attack when she was 54 (*Guardian*, 14 January 2023). In 1997, she had released 'Don't Cry Daddy' as a duet with her father's vocals to mark the 20th anniversary of his death. Here, we can see the hugely significant role of the 'hand in the dark' – where the mark of continual mourning is projected (*what in psychoanalytic parlance would be deemed to be projective identification – JE*) from daughter to father, who is portrayed as crying:

> Today I stumbled from my bed
> With thunder crashing in my head
> My pillow still wet
> From last night tears…
> Daddy, daddy, please laugh again
> Daddy ride us on your back again
> Oh, daddy, please don't cry
> Oh, daddy, please don't cry

And here's a Dad who cried in order to make his 4-year-old granddaughter feel more at ease with her own tears:

> I have a picture in my mind of my very deaf 94-year-old Dad sitting in the garden with Sara – about 2 – both of them drawing pictures and

laughing and scribbling and seeming both to be in the same mood. When Sara tore her picture by mistake and looked as if she was going to cry, Dad did the same and tore up his picture and that became the game. Sara didn't talk much at that age and Dad could never have heard her anyway.

"Finding Her Shape"

A daughter's view of herself through the eyes of the father. This section is written by my colleague, child and adolescent psychotherapist, Alison Roy.

> But from thine eyes my knowledge I derive,
> And, constant stars, in them I read such art
> As truth and beauty shall together thrive
> If from thyself, to store thou wouldst convert
> (William Shakespeare: Sonnet 14)

I approached this theme, said Alison Roy, from the perspective of the daughter, being a daughter myself. However, as Winnicott (1947) explained, 'there is no such thing as a baby', and 'wherever one finds an infant, one finds maternal care, and without maternal care there would be no infant'. I have therefore shifted my focus to exploring the significant role of the father (or paternal figures) in shaping the daughter and influencing the way she sees herself but doing this alongside her other attachments. For every dyad I imagined, I found myself thinking about triads (*see previous chapters – JE*) and every time I thought about a father and daughter – there was a mother. I also felt uncomfortable leaving a daughter with only her father and excluding the mother, just as I used to struggle when working with mothers and their babies in a perinatal team and, despite my best intentions, rarely saw the fathers.

This then is where I will begin – at the beginning, with an infant who is biologically a daughter of two parents – the parental couple.

The baby daughter's shape will change significantly throughout her lifetime, both physically but also psychologically, emotionally and socially. She may even see her gender and core identity as a girl/woman shift, something we are beginning to understand better in the context of these times where there is a little more flexibility around identity and with more power assigned to the individual about how they see themselves and how they wish others to see them. I would therefore like to think about the daughter as a person in these more open terms and times, as someone who may present as (and internalise) both male and female attributes or identities, especially during adolescence.

Here, I will refer to the daughter using 'she' and 'her' pronouns, but I acknowledge that there are biological daughters who no longer identify themselves this way. I will also use the 'he', 'his' and 'him' pronouns when referring to the father, but my intention is not to exclude those same-sex parental relationships where there are paternal and maternal attributes held and provided by both. I would though like to explore more specifically, the role of the father (or a paternal attachment figure) in shaping the daughter's personality, her sense of a separate self and how she chooses to identify herself as she grows into maturity.

In terms of her identity and her sense of where she fits or belongs, a daughter will usually have an idea of herself in relation to the parental couple who brought her into being. This appears to be the case even if she doesn't remember either or both of her birth parents or was removed from them very early on in her life. I have written about this more extensively in terms of the adoptive experience (Roy, 2020). There have now been numerous scientific developments in fertility treatment, meaning that there are different options available to parent or a parental couple who are not able or in a position to conceive through a physical union. Whichever way a child arrives into the world, an idea of the parental couple, the bringing together of two cells (containing much biological and psychological history) and creating the life of a third, is profound. Even for the adopted child who may have a very intimate and positive experience of being parented by their adoptive parents, there remains (*for most – JE*) a powerful fantasy of the original birth couple.

A daughter therefore is not an isolated being, she is born under the eyes of a thousand stars, some of whom have long since died, but their light and influence shine on. Her ancestors have all played a part in her arrival and her story. It is curious then that the eyes of the father seem to hold a particular brightness for a daughter throughout her life.

My Father – passing on an inhibition? A question another female contributor asked:

> My father was an only child whose mother died when he was about 12 years old. Before that she used to sing and he used to accompany her on the piano, so that was quite an intense memory for him.

> When as a young child myself I sang around the house, he used to tell me vehemently to stop: 'You can't sing.' In later life, I always had great difficulty singing, and I don't know if he was right or if he inhibited me! When I was 50, I took singing lessons, and in the lessons, I could sing, but alone now I still can't do it. That self-expression eludes me although I long for it, and I think pleasurable self-expression eluded him. When I was young, he was often working hard, often angry. He married someone who had also lost her mother in childhood, so I imagine they understood some of each other's suffering and loss. They had quite a difficult marriage, as my mother was unhappy, and I don't think he understood that. She could easily, and sometimes, purposefully, annoy him and would seek to make him angry with me. He lost his temper easily, hit me and shook her. I remember one Christmas: they were preparing the lunch in the kitchen, and I was in the sitting room with the relatives.

We heard shouting, and then it went quiet. Later, my Mum told me he had thrown the turkey out of the window on to the lawn. They picked the grass off it and served it. So, I don't think his marriage gave him much joy, and I'm not sure that his children did either. He was a lecturer in engineering and never particularly enjoyed that but worked responsibly and sought additional qualifications; he sat in the dining room for hours studying. What he really liked was making things. He took pleasure working in wood and metal, made furniture for our home, toys for me as a child and fitted cupboards in my flat when I was grown-up. He is long dead now, and I am nearly 80, but I treasure a brass tea caddy shaped like a treasure chest, a copper-lidded pot and a coffee table that he made and a bentwood rocking chair that he mended. What he always insisted was that he was a craftsman, not an artist. I feel I'm not a singer. When I was about 10, he bought an old Lanchester car that didn't run – it had to be towed home. He took the engine out and worked on it at the dining table through the whole winter until he had it working, and we could go out in it. He didn't give up, and I don't either.

After retirement, my Dad went back to college and learned how to make violins. He was painstakingly successful and used his wood and metalwork skills to make special tools that he needed. His workshop held half-finished violins, and various other stringed instruments that he'd made. When I helped them move to a sheltered flat, we kept the house for a year and moved things out slowly. One day I wasn't around, so they took a taxi to the old house to look for something. The taxi driver admired several items and asked for them. They were all given to him, including all the stringed instruments! My Dad didn't think anyone else wanted them. Luckily, I have one of his best violins, which I treasure, and my sister has another. He put our names and our mother's, inside our instruments. The other very sad thing about that is that no one ever played any of them, and my Dad couldn't. He and my mother had clung together all their married lives in spite of their discord and were interdependent. After she died, he became ill and followed her within six months. On his deathbed, he asked me if there was enough money and I reassured him, so he was a responsible provider till the end and deserved to be happier than he was. (*A sad tale indeed, that has haunted his daughter, in the intergenerational way we have learned to understand, so that even at the age of 80, she herself can't sing – JE*)

And now back to Alison Roy's section:
There are a number of research studies which indicate that it is the father or those in a daughter's life who fulfil a paternal function for her, who will play a specific role in the development of her personality and her sense of a separate self. Waddell (1998) writes about the centrality of relationships for personality development and how our early relationships prepare us for later

life disappointments and frustrations: 'The capacity to develop is very much dependent ... on the different degrees to which it is possible to tolerate frustration and absence' (Waddell, 1998, p. 197).

There is also a certain amount of 'shape shifting' of finding a shape that fits, which occurs in adolescence, beautifully articulated by Pullman in the *Northern Lights* trilogy (Pullman, 1995). In these coming-of-age novels, Pullman imagines each individual with a 'daemon' – a visual presentation that takes the form of an animal representing the soul but also helpfully revealing the core personality. Throughout childhood and into early adolescence, the daemon freely shape-shifts and regularly transforms. However, in late adolescence, the personality begins to 'settle', and the shape of the daemon also therefore becomes fixed.

In fictional literature written by women, the father or father figure may be portrayed as mostly protective and benevolent (Austen, Brontë, Eliot), even if he isn't very effective or gets killed off early in the narrative. However, others (Carter, Atwood, Smith, Kingsolver) portray the mother as the most powerful and benevolent force in the life of a young woman and the father or fathers as more predatory and dominant, or at least complicit with misogyny. Much has been made, and rightly so, of the need for secure base in order for an infant, child or young person to thrive. Bowlby's attachment theory has been a useful framework for understanding the parent/infant bond and patterns of how we relate to others and their roots in infancy. A primitive need to have a home and be 'found' is also written about by others: Bion describes the reverie between a parent and infant and the mental processes of alpha functioning or containment (Bion, 1962; 1965); Winnicott (1953; 1960) focuses on the importance of emotional holding or being central in the mother's mind; and Stern (1985) writes about developing a sense of self through being known and understood. Bion also offers us further understanding of the significance of the parent's role in the early social environment, which is to develop 'mental apparatus' (Bion, 1962; 1970), and Klein (1937; 1946) writes about the importance of the parent's role in regulating projective processes and containing primitive anxieties.

The infant defends itself against these by splitting its experiences into good and bad, and it is this aspect of splitting for the daughter that is curious in relation to the father. In my experience of working with parents alongside their children, it is the father (or for same-sex couples, the one who holds more of the paternal function), who usually expresses more of the internal conflict or split in his behaviour towards his daughter. The same father who delights in his daughter can equally become impatient, furious and punishing of her. 'He will big her up one minute and cut her down to size the next', was how one mother described the turbulent relationship between her partner and their teenaged daughter.

The good and bad resources of the father seem to exist predominantly outside the feeding relationship. A mother's desire to feed (*which can last in different ways throughout life – JE*) means that for the infant (and within herself), she possesses both the good and bad breast and has to regulate persecutory and primitive anxieties for the infant and within herself. A father's desire to protect potentially sits alongside the urge to control and possess, the good and bad penis or potency.

The male gaze: are there mixed messages here?

These are very different perspectives of being a man, which are helpful and in encouraging a more balanced view of the father's place in the family, but the societal view of men and the roles they hold can be easily oversimplified or caricatured, as is the case for women. Women or female children are all too often depicted as unpredictable and irrational or 'overly emotional' by men/fathers and even other women/mothers, just for expressing a feeling. Perhaps we are all guilty of oversimplifying things with regards to difference, and in doing so, we marginalise each other when we actually have more in common than we have discernible differences.

For daughters who have not had a safe experience of being with a father or who have encountered many unsafe men in their formative years, it can be difficult to know the difference between those who will care and protect and those who will abuse and/or exploit. In my experience, I have understood how it is much more challenging for these young women to set limits and develop self-protective behaviours, when they have not had a 'good enough' experience of a father or father figures (as well as mother or mother figures) to relate to (Roy, 2024). *(Judith Herman's (1981) book,* Father-Daughter Incest *is a useful study of this distressing theme, which is beyond my remit here – JE)*

John Berger, in his book, *Ways of Seeing* (1977), which was the written text for his BBC series, writes about women and the male gaze: 'A woman must continually watch herself. She is almost continually accompanied by her own image of herself.'

Young women have described their confusion in perceiving that their father wants them to look beautiful but experiencing his apparent fury or disgust when they look desirable, as one adolescent explained: 'He doesn't like me rolling my skirt up when I go to school and hates me wearing makeup, or crop tops but for …'s birthday meal, he yelled at me for wearing jeans and for not making an effort!' Exasperated, she concluded that there was no pleasing him – 'I just can't win.'

This idea of winning or losing the father's approval and confusion is a theme that comes up frequently in my work with young women. I am intrigued by their competitiveness with each other, not apparently for the real father (although there are similarities here with sibling rivalry) but for an imagined or idealised version of the father who never seems to be satisfied. In this respect, a daughter has learned to see herself through the eyes of the father or other men (like or unlike her father) to define her image and shape, but she may also have learned to be wary of her 'sisters' and their envy, while not being completely clear of what is and isn't acceptable. This constant pressure will have an impact on the daughters' psychosexual development and potentially contaminate the nurturing and loving 'eyes' of the father with an expectation of desire, rivalry with other women and introducing a more erotic element to a girl's relationship with her father.

Berger (1977) again makes a similar point: 'One might simplify this by saying: men act and women appear. Men look at women. Women watch themselves being looked at. Thus she turns herself into an object – and most particularly an object of vision: a sight.'

Scopophilia was a psychoanalytic concept created by Sigmund Freud to describe the pleasure in looking, or what is more usually known as voyeurism. It is widely used in film studies, for obvious reasons, particularly by feminist scholars, to describe cinema's popularity as an artistic medium, where women become the objects of male gaze. (Sigmund Freud used the term *scopophilia* to describe, analyse, and explain the concept of *Schaulust*, the pleasure in looking.) The theoretic bases of scopophilia were developed by the psychoanalyst Otto Fenichel, in special reference to the process and stages of psychological identification. That, in developing a personal identity, 'a child, who is looking for libidinous purposes ... wants to look at an object in order [for it] to "feel along with him"'. The impersonal interaction of scopophilia (between the looker and the one looked-at) sometimes replaces personal interactions in the psychological life of a person who is socially anxious, and seeks to avoid feelings of guilt. Lacan's conceptual development of *the gaze* linked the pleasure of scopophilia to the person's apprehension of the Other (person) who is not the Self; that is: 'The gaze is this object lost, and suddenly re-found, in the conflagration of shame, by the introduction of the Other.' The practice of scopophilia is how a person's *desire* is captured by the imaginary representation of the Other. Theories alternative to Lacan's interpretations of scopophilia and the gaze proposed that a child's discovery of genital difference, and the accompanying anxiety about not knowing the difference of the Other sex, form the experience that subsequently impels the child's scopic drive to fulfil the desire to look and to be looked at.

An example can be seen in *The Memoirs of a Woman of Pleasure* (1749), in which the protagonist Fanny Hill gives her scopophilic observations of two men copulating anally, which include descriptions of the furnishings and the *décor* of the room:

> at length I observed a paper patch of the same colour as the wainscot, which I took to conceal some flaw; but then it was so high that I was obliged to stand upon a chair to reach it, which I did, as soft as possible, and, with a point of a bodkin, soon pierced it, and opened myself espial room sufficient. And now, applying my eye close, I commanded the room perfectly, and could see my two young sparks romping and pulling one another about, entirely, to my imagination, in frolic and innocent play.

Similar to Berger, feminists argue that it is predominantly a patriarchal societal view of a girl and then a woman, which makes it very difficult for her to see herself as she could be. She has been conditioned to understand her shape through the eyes of a man – the first man to shape her being her father. In her book, *Rage Becomes Her*, Chemaly (2018) writes about how women are seen by men, beginning with the father. She argues that girls are taught from birth by their fathers not to express themselves openly and to suppress their anger.

Freud used a Greek myth to explore feelings of exclusion or inclusion that the triad or threesomes generate along with the accompanying envy and competition. However, in this way, the baby develops a self and a couple in mind, as we have suggested earlier.

Winnicott looks at this process for the infant, both male and female, and the infant's needs for an accurate reflection. If the eyes of the mother (or other) reflect back a distorted view, there will be a negative effect on their development but beyond the dyad is the safety and reassurance offered by the third, the triad which includes the other parent. If the maternal reflection is distorted, the paternal presence could offer a more grounded and accurate impression for her to get hold of, and vice versa (see Fonagy, 2001).

Roy expands on these ideas within the context of our times and the arrival of social media: There have been significant changes over the last century in the way we see and present ourselves to others. We have moved from painting portraits to taking photos with cameras, then cameras became digital so that images could be shared with others electronically. Then came the arrival of smart phones and with them, a whole new world of reportage and self-disclosure. Now almost anyone in the western world can be a photographer, a news reporter but also a critic and a voyeur. With just a touch of a screen we can capture an image for 'the world' to see via social media platforms on the world wide web. We have therefore entered a more narcissistic version of society where we spend more time looking at our own reflections than noticing those and the world around us. We, or more significantly, our children may well miss more genuine opportunities for connection and intimacy. The 2024 Association of Child Psychotherapists explored the digital age from a digital perspective in their conference. Can we maintain connection and intimacy via digital portals? The image of the self is viewed and appraised on a grand scale and in very public forums, and rather than having the idea of benevolent ancestors looking down on her from the stars, our daughters are being subjected to an ever-present scrutiny and judgement from god-like mortals: be it their peers, bosses, extended families, potential friends, lovers and enemies. This predicament, because that it what it is, is also profound when we think about the development of a child who longs to be seen and accepted by the father.

Roy said she had encountered a number of adopted young women whose response to this longing is to put themselves at risk by meeting older men in chat rooms, sharing images of themselves and then arranging to meet them in person even though on one level they know they will be abused and exploited. Adoptive parents and professional networks may try in vain to prevent this from happening, but every time a device is removed, another appears or they find a different way to make contact.

In conversation with some of these young women in a group session, one member of the group explained that all her life she had tried to find her birth father. 'He could be out there just waiting for me,' she told me. 'I have to look my best, as one day it could be him.'

Another of these young women talked about her loneliness and despair because she felt that she was 'the wrong shape'. She described how many of her peers looked the same, they were skinny and blonde, and she felt excluded because she appeared different and struggled to recognise her beauty or worth, for she could not meet the criteria for a conventional beauty. I found it hard to establish where this so-called version of beauty came from. It seemed to come as much from other women as it did from men, but what was evident was that each of these young women would go to great lengths to be noticed and appraised as 'pretty' by men, but especially by those men who were old enough to be their fathers.

This is a complicated picture, as these adopted young women recalled that as small children they had been encouraged to present themselves as 'cute' or 'pretty' when photographed for adoption magazines and adopter recruitment events. (*sadly, an all-too-common event, so that would-be adoptive parents are surprised and dismayed by the 'real' child they eventually welcome into their family – JE*) The young women saw that presenting this version of themselves was a necessary part of securing 'forever parents'. This pressure to be seen as desirable in order to belong and be accepted continued into their adolescence and early adulthood.

Unfortunately, I have seen similar patterns emerging in the behaviour of other young women more generally, perhaps not with the same level of risk and potential for exploitation, but concerning, nonetheless. My contributor was shocked to learn from a 15-year-old that she and her friends used filters and apps in order to make themselves look thinner, younger, taller, smaller, or they could shrink their waists and enlarge their eyes, lips and breasts. They were seeking a version of beauty for themselves that involved changing their shape, airbrushing out imperfections and hiding behind so-called 'perfection'. However, they also described feeling invisible, exposed or unacknowledged and the exhaustion of presenting themselves constantly for the eyes of the world to appraise, accept or reject. This was taking its toll on their sense of themselves and their ability to relax and be in the moment.

There is healing power of the natural world, as an environment which can support new life, growth and recovery. There are many podcasts now online which talk of the beneficial aspect of walking 'in nature'. 'The metaphor of the garden is useful when thinking more positively about what a daughter needs from her father. To begin with he, like a gardener has a role in preparing the soil and tending to the first shoots of new life, but later on as she matures, she will want her own space or 'a bit of earth'. The gardener therefore, like a good-enough father, keeps a watchful eye over the garden but feels pride and delight when the garden takes on a life of its own and blossoms, or when the child herself wants to be a gardener, too. There is also room within this metaphor for a maternal or nurturing presence working in partnership with the attentive father/gardener or burgeoning daughter/gardener. Wilke (2019) writes, 'Stories, fairy tales, and myths help evolve a sense of self in each member of a community an identity integrating a feeling of "who I am" and "who we are"' (p. 205). There is a story explored in more depth in *A for Adoption* (Roy, 2020). *The Secret Garden* by Frances Hodgson Burnett (1911) narrates a journey of discovery for a child called Mary, but also for her 'father' figure (Mary's uncle) by using the metaphor of the garden. Mary arrives from India to live with her uncle but has little understanding of how to connect to others and no memory at all of the parental couple. Her dead parents took no interest in her while they were alive, and she has little sense of 'uncle', the absent father figure. However, during her stay, she begins to build healthy relationships. She meets Dickon, a boy who is full of life and treats her as an equal. He has no expectations for her to be anything other than a child like himself, with a strong attachment to others and to the natural world. At the point in the story when Mary finds the secret garden, she has become more joyfully alive, parented by her peers but also 'fed and nurtured' by the natural world. She has become aware of herself as a living being. Spurred on by her cousin Colin, who has been hidden away because his father feared he was 'damaged', they claim the garden, a place where life begins, for themselves. They are all 'waking up', as if from a deep sleep, with the arrival of spring. Mary's observation of the absent father, her uncle Mr. Craven, is keen, and she notices that his disability is of his own creation. She also recognises how unhappiness has altered him: 'He was not ugly. His face would have been handsome if it had not been so miserable.'

Roy relates how she witnessed how a child coming to life psychologically can inadvertently help to restore colour and purpose to a stuck or despairing parent. When a parent is supported or willing to learn and change, a child can be an insightful teacher. Mary is determined to show her uncle that life is worth living and that she wants to 'make things grow'. In doing so, she reminds Mr. Craven of his late wife and of the woman he loved who tended to the garden but who also had the power within her to create. Mary asks him, falteringly, if she can have 'a bit of earth' to 'make things grow'. His response is warm: 'take it, child, and make it come alive.'

The father figure in *The Secret Garden* discovered his potential as a parent, despite his previous failings, with the help of a vibrant 'daughter' willing him to find his way back to the garden, where he comes face to face not only with the children, full of vitality and joy, but also with the child within himself. To the children, it feels as though the playful and responsive father has finally come home to them and can see them as they really are and need to be. He listens to the children as they tell him their story of how they came to life in the garden: 'The listener laughed until tears came into his eyes, and sometimes tears came into his eyes when he was not laughing.'

In writing about fathers and daughters, Roy feels she has come full circle and back to the beginning, to a garden where the father finds his shape within the triad and can see himself as connected to the mother more clearly through the eyes of his daughter. The daughter in turn sees herself as someone who can bring joy and life to others and, in doing so, is reminded of her own vitality and becomes less preoccupied by her shape and by the approval of others. She is therefore able to internalise the protective and nurturing couple as a model for her own developing relationships. John Berger wrote: 'We never look at just one thing; we are always looking at the relation between things and ourselves.'

Waddell (2002) emphasises the importance of this and having an available presence who can be authentic and self-aware:

> The opportunity to know oneself, and hence to develop as oneself, requires the availability of a presence which has qualities of receptiveness and responsiveness, based in self-knowledge and in a sense of inner worlds which are honest, not counterfeit.
>
> (p. 37)

Roy wanted to end with an example of her own relationship with her father who is a retired head teacher. 'Whenever I challenge him or we are talking about something difficult, he will say, "I just need to put another table leg on the fire."' I have come to understand this to mean that he knows things are cooling between us and that there is tension, but he doesn't know what to do about it, so we have both also learned to say, 'for another time'.

References

Baker Miller, J. (ed.). (1973). *Psychoanalysis and women*. Pelican Original.
Berger, J. (1977) *Ways of seeing*. Penguin.
Bion, W. R. (1962). *Learning from experience*. William Heinemann.
Bion, W. R. (1965). *Experiences in groups and other papers*. Tavistock Publications.
Bion, W. R. (1970). *Attention and interpretation*. Tavistock Publications.
Bodichon, B. (1866). *Reasons for the enfranchisement of women*. Chambers of the Social Science Association.
Chemaly, S. (2018). *Rage becomes her*. Simon & Schuster UK.
Fonagy, P. (2001). *Attachment theory and psychoanalysis*. Routledge.
Gatens, M. (1991). *Feminism and philosophy: Perspectives on difference and equality*. Indiana University Press.
Herman, J. L. (1981). *Father-daughter incest*. Harvard University Press.
Hodgson Burnett, F. (1911). *The secret garden*. Frederick A. Stokes.
Klein, M. (1937). *Love, guilt and reparation: And other works 1921–1945*. Hogarth Press.
Klein, M. (1946). *Envy and gratitude*. Hogarth Press.
Mill, J. S. (1869). *The subjection of women*. Longmans Green.
Pullman, P. (1995). *Northern lights*. Scholastic Point.
Roy, A. (2020). *A for adoption: An exploration of the adoption experience for families and professionals*. Routledge.

Roy, A. (2024) Under the eyes of a thousand stars, Open Door, https://www.theopendoorlewes.com/blog/2024/7/26/under-the-eyes-of-a-thousand-stars-by-alison-roy#:~:text=Alison%20Roy%20explains%20how%20fathers,should%20look%2C'%20she%20insists.

Stern, D. N. (1985). *The interpersonal world of the infant: A view from psychoanalysis and developmental psychology*. Basic Books.

Waddell, M. (1998). *Inside lives: Psychoanalysis and the growth of the personality*. Routledge.

Waddell, M. (2002). *Inside lives: Psychoanalysis and the growth of the personality* (2nd ed.). Routledge.

Wilke, L. D. (2019) *The alchemy of noise*. She Writes Press.

Winnicott, D. W. (1947). The squiggle game. In *The collected works of D. W. Winnicott*, eds L. Caldwell and H. Taylor Robinson (vol. 8). Oxford University Press.

Winnicott, D. W. (1953). *The child, the family, and the outside world*. Penguin Books.

Winnicott, D. W. (1960). The theory of the parent-infant relationship. *International Journal of Psychoanalysis, 41*, 585–595.

5 Do Siblings Remember Fathers Differently?

While there has been 'one father' externally, do these fathers become differently remembered, inside each child's mind? What we need to do is balance alertness to the way inner unconscious fantasy influences the perception of 'the object' and relationship to it, with an awareness that each person has, stored in the mind, experiences with a real parent who has particular qualities, strengths and shortcomings. The Van Gogh brothers had the same father, but reacted differently to him, in a sense, they had two different fathers. Their father was a pastor of the Dutch Reformed Church, and wanted Vincent to follow in his footsteps, Vincent had a go at being a pastor, but he was not very good at it, then he was given oil paints by his brother, and wanted to be an artist. He also wanted to please his father but did not know how. His 'modern ideas' came into conflict with his parents' more stereotyped ideas, and in 1881, he was asked to leave home – or he left of his own volition. 'I sent these drawings to Pa so he could see I am doing something', was his heartfelt cry. He did try. And, yes, he was driven demented. Theo, an art dealer, the younger brother, was less recalcitrant, and had a relationship with a very different father. He became Vincent's 'wise brother' and set him on the path to becoming an artist – never recognised in his lifetime but now one of the most celebrated (and commercially valued) artists in the world. Vincent van Gogh wanted to make his father Theodorus van Gogh proud of him. But Vincent felt he disappointed his father, a pastor, by giving up his ambition to become a preacher. Vincent hoped to become a respected artist instead, but his father died in 1885 and never saw his son exhibited at major art expositions from 1888 onwards. If only his father had known.

The novelist Honoré de Balzac (1799–1850) was also intended by his lawyer father (who had been born into peasant stock) to become a lawyer himself. After a traumatic time in boarding school, where he had a breakdown, he tried being a lawyer for a few years, to fit in with what his father wanted, but gave up and went bankrupt as a printer, then went on to write 85 novels in 20 years. So here is another example of the father whose wishes needed to be ignored. Honoré de Balzac's relationship with his father, Bernard-François Balzac, was complex and often strained. Bernard-François, a man of peasant stock who rose to become a civil servant during the Napoleonic era, had high

DOI: 10.4324/9781003521846-6

expectations for his son. He was strict, ambitious and had a strong sense of discipline, which he imposed on his family. Balzac's father sent him to rigorous schools, including the Oratorian College in Vendôme, where the young Balzac experienced harsh discipline and eventually had a breakdown. This period left a lasting impact on him, influencing the themes of authority and power in his later works. Despite the pressure and strict upbringing, Bernard-François did support Balzac financially during his early career, even though he disapproved of his son's decision to become a writer, which he saw as financially unstable and socially risky.

The tension between father and son was exacerbated by Balzac's repeated failures and financial troubles. Nevertheless, the elder Balzac's ambition and determination to improve his family's social standing probably influenced Honoré's own relentless drive and prolific output as a writer. The relationship was marked by a mixture of support and disapproval, reflecting the broader societal pressures and personal ambitions that shaped Balzac's life and work.

Here again, the passions of the child emerge after he himself has emerged from the controlling desires of his father, whereas many of his siblings did indeed fit in with father's wishes: as Cat Stevens, the singer, said, he was not given a space to be listened to. 'I had to go away.' The novelist Henry James nevertheless called Balzac 'the father of us all'. There is no record of what Balzac himself had to say about emerging from his father's control, unlike his siblings, who would have had a different view.

Here, we have an example of one father, two perspectives and to flesh out this reasoning are two siblings' recollections, followed by the recollections of the sister who was born between them:

My father was 87 when he died. We spent about 10 or 11 years together when he could have been 'Daddy'. He was in his own way. Once I was sitting on my heels outside my grandfather's saw mills, stroking a donkey's head inclined towards me and he took a photograph. He was very good at photographs and made images that others admired. He had his own dark room where he would retreat to develop his photographs. I would sometimes go with him and watch the images emerge out of the fluid in the trays where he placed the special paper. And then, there was the enlarger which worked its magic. He has many cameras and especially prized, a Leica. But it is this picture – just this one of the many, many he must have taken of us as children, which gives me a Daddy feeling. That day, that donkey at the mill, my father, was very present. I still have it.

I remember the smell of his handkerchief, musty, snotty, male when he wiped my face when it was dirty. I remember his voice on the radio when he gave his talks, his calm when I was hurt, which was often. But, was he ever there, really there? He had nothing in his past to put him in touch with the needs of his children. (*He had been born 'illegitimately'* and even at his own mother's funeral, he said he was her nephew ...) He was a bit stumped by thinking about his children's needs. And then it was too late. I slipped away (i.e., left my South American home) and was left with a picture of a little boy stroking a donkey. I was his son, but I would never be his child again. In its own quiet way, his life had taken a curious course and made him a parent. He was in a way a civil servant of life who in late retirement grew flowers in my sister's London garden, listened to music and read Trollope. He did not seem troubled by the unmapped interior of himself, which perhaps, he long ago decided not to explore. He had a melancholic seam, and one of his favourite books was *Religio Medici*.

A contemporary reviewer described it as follows:

> A new little volume has arrived from Holland entitled *Religio Medici* written by an Englishman and translated into Latin by some Dutchman. It is a strange and pleasant book, but very delicate and wholly mystical; the author is not lacking in wit and you will see in him quaint and delightful thoughts. There are hardly any books of this sort. If scholars were permitted to write freely we would learn many novel things, never has there been a newspaper to this; in this way the subtlety of the human spirit could be revealed.

I have it now on my shelf. Maybe he was looking for the subtlety of the human spirit. I don't think he found it in that sparsely populated country on the north coast of South America that was his home for 30 years. He was also much taken by the book of Job. Was Job a pessimist? The book of Job is among the other Old Testament books both a philosophical riddle and a historical riddle. Controversy has long raged about which parts of this epic belong to its original scheme and which were added at a considerably later date. When you deal with any ancient artistic creation, it is important to understand that it grew gradually. The book of Job may have grown gradually just as Westminster Abbey grew gradually. But the people who made the original story, like the people who made Westminster Abbey, did not attach much importance to the actual date and the actual author.

Without going into questions of unity as understood by scholars, we may say of the scholarly riddle that the book has unity in the sense that all great traditional creations have unity. There is a real sense in which the book of Job stands apart from most of the books included in the canon of the Old Testament. Job was a patient man, bearing all his tribulations with resilience and fortitude. The book of Job stands definitively alone because the Job asks, 'But what is the purpose of God? Is it worth the sacrifice even of our miserable humanity? Of course, it is easy enough to wipe out our own paltry wills for the sake of a will that is grander and kinder. But is it grander and kinder? Let God use His tools; let God break His tools. But what is He doing, and what are they being broken for?'

The importance of the book of Job can't be expressed adequately even by saying that it is the most interesting of ancient books. We may almost say too that it is the most interesting of modern books. In truth, of course, neither of the two phrases covers the matter, because fundamental human religion and fundamental human irreligion are both at once old and new; philosophy is either eternal or it is not philosophy. Job does not in any sense look at life in a gloomy way. If wishing to be happy and being quite ready to be happy constitutes an optimist, Job is an optimist. He is a perplexed optimist; he is an exasperated optimist; he is an outraged and insulted optimist. He wishes the universe to justify itself. The book of Job is chiefly remarkable, for the fact that it doesn't end in a way that is conventionally satisfactory. Job is not told that his misfortunes were due to his sins or a part of any plan for his improvement. But in the prologue, we see Job tormented not because he was the worst of men, but because he was the best. It is the lesson of the whole work that man is most comforted by paradoxes. This father, seen to be interested in Job's book, is seen by one sibling to be 'untroubled by the unmapped interior of himself which perhaps, he long ago decided not to explore'.

And here are his brother's more 'factual' recollections:

Most of the time Dad was 4,000 miles away, so my memories of him are of being young (up to age 12) in South America, then on their visits to the UK every three years and, finally, when they retired to London. Until they retired to London, contact was by the then usual letter form. I cannot say that this was an ideal way of keeping in touch. We moved from Guyana to Brazil in 1944 when I was three and my brother scarcely one and moved back in 1949, by which time I had two sisters. My early schooling at the *Progresso Brazileiro* was in Portuguese, but my father was assiduous in making sure that I was also speaking and reading English. With hindsight, I can see what a marvellous father he was in many ways; kind, considerate and caring. I wonder to what extent this was the result of him being so aware of not having a father and having had a distant relationship with his mother (*see earlier comment*), especially when he was very young. I was not a model son, always getting into one scrape or another and frequently needing to be bailed out financially. To the extent that he once wrote to me starting, 'I am depressed, your mother is depressed ...', enumerating the reasons.

I have no memory of negative interactions with my parents. *(Could we think that these may have been repressed?- JE)* I think I and my siblings were so lucky having the parents we had. They even dealt with the difficulty of dealing with Mrs Smith, my landlady in Burgess Hill where I was staying when she found me in bed with her daughter. We set up home at the age of 19 in London and were happy for a number of years until she formed a disastrous relationship with another man. When I had finished my advanced studies in 1966, I was welcomed home for some R and R. Dad could not face the celebrations marking the end of colonial rule, and he and I and my cousin Lawrence went to stay at Dadanawa, a ranch in the Guyanese interior with family connections. That was an enjoyable occasion which I shared with him: warm memories. When I returned to London, I met my future wife, and we were married in 1968. They were not able to make it to the wedding but were very supportive. In 1969, they retired to the UK and rented in Bayswater until they received the money from the sale of our house in Guyana and bought a flat in East Putney. Through all of this, they were always supportive and especially when my marriage ended. I went to stay with them until I had bought a house in Wandsworth. Again, nothing but understanding from my father. When I met someone who would be my partner for 18 years, they were again totally supportive, treating her as a daughter and welcoming her children. I wonder if unconsciously my father was remembering his childhood and making sure that I (and my siblings) had the love and care from him that had been so sadly missing in his life. My partner and I would often go round to their flat in Wimbledon, which they moved into when they sold the flat in Putney. Mother became increasingly frail, and Dad became chief cook and bottle-washer and carer, making sure that she went for walks with him.

When personal circumstances caused them to find a new flat in Sutton, father again looked after our mother in an exemplary way. It must have been so stressful for him.

In 1983, Jill decided that she did not want to spend the rest of her life with someone who was wedded to his job and worked long hours, leaving little over for her. At the same time, I was fired, but my partner had already moved out. I then went to live and work in Guyana. While I was there, mummy died in October 1986. I came over for the funeral. At this point, Dad decided that he had nothing to live for and went into a decline. It was a depressing situation for us all, but he would not listen to our pleas and basically decided to check out with a bottle of whisky. Depressingly, there was nothing we could do to change his mind, and he died in March 1987. During this sad time, my brother and sister-in-law kept him company on a daily basis. (*And he did still have some sense of himself left: the sister-in-law left the photos she had taken in his drawer as he said he did not want to see them ... she returned for something she had forgotten, and he was eagerly looking at them – JE*) I was sorry that I could not be there at that time for him. I can only think that when he felt that there was nothing useful that he could now do for his children, he had the right to check out, even though we did not want him to. Patient Job indeed. 'What luck to have such a father as a model. I hope I can be half as good a father to my two girls.' The youngest of these two girls is now 21, ... what would she say?

So we have two narratives here – snapshots you might say of a father coming out of the developing fluid: the same father, but different memories. The second is more of a factual account, with feelings hinted at occasionally but not spelt out. 'What luck to have such a father as a model.' The first account is one that delves more deeply into the internal world of a father who had had no models of how to interact at a feeling level with his sons. 'Born "illegitimately", he had been farmed out at an early age, taught to call his mother his aunt.' But, was he ever there, really there? He had nothing in his past to put him in touch with the needs of his children. He was a bit stumped by it.

And then it was too late…

In the book of Job, as I have indicated, the problem of human pain confronts the person of God. The book leads to the conclusion that God's goodness and greatness deserve and demand our love and worship. Two snapshots emerging from the developing fluid. And here are the memories of their sister, born between the two boys, not mentioned by either of them:

> Our father was on the whole a quiet man, but growing up, I always felt secure in his love for us all. I felt that we were his life. One funny memory that has stuck with me is of me sitting at the table in my parents' bedroom, struggling with maths homework and feeling his exasperation when I couldn't understand what he was trying to explain to me! I was always useless at maths! I also spent much time with him in his darkroom – he took lots of photos of us, and it was wonderful watching the images appear in the tray of chemicals. I have sad memories of how distant he became with my mother as they aged, and he found it difficult to accept the changes in her when she was no longer her active, talkative and cheerful self. I think he was quite cruel then, but I understood that he just didn't know how to cope and so retired to his books and classical music. I loved and respected him – he never raised his voice when I misbehaved – one of his looks was enough. In my mind, I still talk to him and my mother every day.

Sibling rivalry does not get a mention here, and yet it is powerfully at work in unconscious fantasies (Mitchell, 2003). Melanie Klein (1957) comments that a residue of schizoid and paranoid feelings split off from the rest of the personality can be found to be common if otherwise fairly 'normal' people (p. 117).

And here are the baby's recollections, though she is now in her seventies:

> I remember my father as a quiet gentle man. My mother was definitely the one who ruled our little roost. Dad was so patient and was always

willing to help me with my homework. He was highly intelligent and a former teacher. When I would ask him permission to do something, he would always say, 'Ask your mother'. Now I wish I had asked him so many unanswered questions, but when you're very young, there's always tomorrow to do so. My memories of him are very good, and I'm happy he was able to have a family life with us, as he didn't have one himself.

References

Klein, M. (1957). *Envy and gratitude*. Tavistock Publications.
Mitchell, J. (2003). *Siblings: Sex and violence*. Polity Press.

6 Handing on in Identification, and Letting Go…Chh-Ch-Ch-Changes…

The poet Seamus Heaney identified with the skill and expertise of his father, in using a spade, in the poem, 'Digging' (Heaney, 1966). Their work may have been very different, and Heaney in this poem is quite disparaging about his own work, and gives us a detailed description of the process of digging, while acknowledging that, unlike his father and his grandfather, he is not 'a digger'. And yet he is…

> Between my finger and my thumb
> The squat pen rests; snug as a gun.
> …
> I'll dig with it.

As he surely does, 'setting the darkness echoing' with his poems about his youth, as I too did with the memoir, *Pieces of Molly* (Gurney, 2012).

Keep the questions rolling. Rather like the poodle in the park, who was not interested in the static ball, but raced after the same ball enthusiastically once it was thrown, let's keep the ideas evolving. What do boys need? Positive father role models for boys can have a profound impact on their development. A recent Radio 4 programme called 'The Boys Are Not All Right' waves some red flags. In a website called 'Fatherly', some nouns are suggested for what fathers may be: provider, protector, leader, teacher, helper, enabler, friend. Perhaps we may agree with some of these and disagree with others. Cat Stevens who was 'ordered to listen' would not be in agreement with 'teacher', for instance. Atticus Finch in *To Kill a Mockingbird* was known for his integrity, wisdom and compassion; Atticus Finch exemplifies moral strength and teaches valuable life lessons to his children. Mufasa in the *Lion King* is a symbol of strength, wisdom and paternal love. He imparts important values to Simba, teaching him about responsibility and leadership. Despite his unconventional methods, Daniel Hillard in *Mrs Doubtfire* is portrayed as a loving and devoted father who ultimately prioritises his children's happiness by disguising himself as a female housekeeper. Based on a true story, Chris Gardner's determination, following an early life marked by homelessness and other significant struggles, recounted in *The Pursuit of Happyness*, shows unwavering love for his son, which exemplifies the sacrifices fathers make for their children. If you believe in something, he declares, follow it through (Gardner, 2006).

These characters offer diverse examples of positive father figures, each contributing valuable lessons and inspiration to boys and audiences alike. Identification is a core concept here.

> Italo Svevo, the writer and businessman, had developed a migraine. His father used to get them often too. The more time went on, the more he resembled him, in ailments as well; the moment had come to do as he had done and follow him, to go over his steps again quickly, yes, to shorten distances visibly.
>
> (Magris, 1997, p. 269)

Svevo was concerned to reach 'the end' in his identification with his father, but it was a fractured end. So how can we find the benign Father?

During the 1990s, as one of my psychoanalytic colleagues relates:

> I set up a CAMHS (Child and Adolescent Mental Health Service) service for army families. This began life as a conventional under-fives service built upon the Tavistock remit of an assessment and five sessions for families, and where on referral the lead child was under the age of five. However, the level of emotional deprivation within these invariably traumatised families meant that, for a great many of them, the five session part of the remit soon became re-negotiated as open-ended.

> One of the obvious issues to influence the initial presentations of the child was the poor parenting received, from traumatised parents. This was poor for several reasons. Fathers were often away on dangerous exercises or facing action in one of the World's trouble spots. Wives (invariably in these cases, the parents were heterosexual and married) were not allowed to be in touch with their husbands while they were away. Along with their own anxieties, they needed to attempt to contain their children's. For some operations, they were not allowed to speak with other wives, including those who were neighbours. On their return, fathers were forbidden to speak to friends, wives and other family members about where they had been, and what they had done and seen there. (This had been the pattern set by World War II, where returning soldiers had morphed into men at home who discussed nothing of their now repressed traumatic experiences.) The homecoming was therefore one in which, after the initial expression of pleasure, family members tended to go silent, as that which they were desperate to speak about was not there to discuss. This specialist CAMHS tried to be flexible in order to offer interventions that were tailored to each family's particular need. In most cases, after a brief piece of work to help the parents attend better to their child's communications, the parents were offered a

longer-term piece of work to enable them to better understand their relationship as a couple, and as a parental couple. In nearly all cases, these couples had become a partnership through an unconscious fit between them largely based upon sharing a similar internal father. For both of them, there was a preoccupation with this father, such that neither was able to offer containment to each other, themselves as individuals, or to their children. In many cases, this resulted in a very dangerous family life. Ordinary stresses and strains were not understood for being such. When the trauma of not knowing about the father's army work (children and wives), and the trauma experienced carrying out these duties were added, family life so often became aggressive, violent and abusive for fathers, mothers and children.

Here was one couple for whom psychotherapy was a success. Both had external fathers who had been violent towards them as children and adolescents. Both had an internal parental couple that featured an almost invisible internal mother dominated by a threatening internal father. Army life provides many such couples the promise of escape and asylum from these experiences with their families of origin. However, the extent of asylum is extremely limited and certainly does not stretch to being an effective-enough container. The clinical work enabled both parents to address their identification with a violent internal father. Through this, they were able to find a more benign paternal object, one that enabled a better relationship, and through this, a containing parental object within themselves as individuals, as a couple and as parents to their children. I think the fact of my being a male psychotherapist may have been a decisive factor in this couple's engagement with me and the work's success.

Fathers themselves need to change over time: it is indeed a long and winding road. Being the father of a baby is very different from being the father of a toddler, of a latency child, of an adolescent. Some questions often asked by me and my colleagues, when working with families: How were you as an adolescent? What worked? What didn't work? What was the best solution at any given time? I (JE) recall a family I saw where the adolescent son was breaking windows, in school and beyond. I asked the whole family to come, and the father explained how he cleaned up the son's sports-bag, throwing out the equipment he didn't need, as well as the dirty socks. When I queried this, the father seemed surprised, and at the suggestion, tentative on my part, that it might be better to let the son, now a teenager, to do this for himself. The father had not found it easy to make the change, from being the father of a latency child who needed some looking after, to being the father of an adolescent son who might gradually be encouraged to look after himself. The father seemed to have no recall of his own father, and how he had been at this vulnerable time. Adolescence is a time of trauma for the individual, trying to make sense of a new self, a changing body, a changing mind, reworking infantile conflicts about rivalry and separation, and working out who to be in the world. It would be satisfying and indeed rather 'magical' if this conversation with the family had led to a change in behaviour on the part of the son immediately, but over time, he started to change, to look after himself, without having to break out of a constraining situation, symbolised by the broken windows. There were changes happening all around. The family continued to attend sessions and were quietly surprised by how talking and thinking together did begin to change the picture.

This may make questions spring to mind. As Bion said, 'It is important to keep your questions in good repair.' It is important to be open to various thoughts here. As a cybernetician friend so aptly put it: 'What Bion is talking about is that to know something, one must first not know it, in order to open up a reflective space for the knowledge to emerge.' Melanie Klein's patients could be pulled from their narcissistic envelope over time and analysis to have a kinder view of their parents. In a narcissistic personality, the subject inserts the self into the traumatising agent, producing identification with the aggressor, as Anna Freud said; the separation between 'normal' projective identification or empathic sharing and intrusiveness is a fine one, as Irma Pick suggested. A patient's view of internal objects can be felt to be either over-identified or distant and harsh, not able to take in experience (Pick, 2018, p. 28). The analyst may need an outside person, such as a 'father' or partner, to provide support, to encourage the analyst to have the strength to hold feelings of hatred for the parasitic patient-baby while having concern for the needy defective baby in the patient. Here again, we have the notion of three-ness, which is at the heart of the Oedipal situation. This idea about hatred of the patient was first elaborated by Winnicott (1949) in his article, 'Hate and the Counter-Transference'. The actual death of a father may be experienced as confirmation of the child's omnipotent murderousness, and the patient may be united with a tyrannical father. (See discussion of Plath's poem in Chapter 12.) A former student of mine, a gay woman now unsurprisingly in a gay marriage, describes choosing her father for identification, going from imitation to identification; she talks about sawing wood in the woodshed and stopping to groan 'Oh, my back', as he did.

> My dad was a working-class lad from Liverpool. Born in the 1920s, he went to school until he turned 11, followed by a long pause. In the late 1940s, he joined the Royal Air Force. He didn't fly because he only had one eye that he could see from. He held the highest security clearance, and we still, to this day, do not know what he actually did beyond 'communications'. I was the youngest of five, born in 1969, while all my siblings had been born in the fifties. My eldest sisters describe the father of their childhoods being good and kind, but sexist. (*Here again we have different impressions, different memories – JE*) But dad was different with me. Perhaps he'd been worn down by the four children that

preceded me, three of whom were girls. I was an agitated and inquisitive child who needed to understand the workings of everything: the car, the lawnmower, the telephone, the radio, the TV, a lock on a door, an air rifle, the hot water heater, any gears, all pulley systems – the list of my obsessions is extremely long, but my dad indulged all of them. Once, after discovering that I was experimenting with the explosive charge of World War II rifle bullets that I'd collected from a nearby munitions dump, and some shotgun gunpowder I'd nicked from a farm, he even showed me how to make a cannon. I still have a shard of World War II bullet casing embedded in my hand after one exploded during my early experiments before dad stepped in to instruct me.

Politics begins in the nursery, as Kraemer said, and the need for identification through imitation is key to this process. In the memoir *Pieces of Molly: An Ordinary Life* (Gurney, 2012), I talked about needing to see my dad as warlike, even though most of my memories of him were much more gentle, as he brought fallen birds in under his coat, and fed the spitting wildcat kittens who lurked under the beams of the sheds (p. 42). Patiently, he stood and pushed the swing higher and higher, so that his daughter could feel she burst out of this terrestrial world to something higher, purer, in ecstasy. 'I rhyme to set the darkness echoing', said the late poet Seamus Heaney, and I too found out by writing *Pieces of Molly* how the darkness could indeed echo.

So where are we now? Perhaps it would be helpful here if I summarise the points I have made so far. What I hope to have shown is that the idea of 'fathers' is of relatively recent origin and that imitation precedes identification. We use words, both in poetry and prose, to open new doors of understanding.

References

Gardner, C. (2006). *The pursuit of happyness*. Amistad.
Gurney, J. (2012). *Pieces of Molly: An ordinary life*. Karnac Books.
Heaney, S. (1966). Digging. In *Death of a naturalist*. Faber and Faber.
Magris, C. (1997). *Microcosms*. Harvill Press.
Pick, I. (2018). *Authenticity in the psychoanalytic encounter*. Routledge.
Winnicott, D. W. (1949). Hate in the counter-transference. *International Journal of Psychoanalysis*, *30*(4), 69–74.

7 Having 'No Father'

The Absent Father and the Single Parent

Let's start with another conundrum: having no father, as this contributor experienced, or having two – this is another turn of the Rubik's cube, and one which produced a different result:

> It is a strange experience, writing something about my father. For a long time, I had no father. Then I had two. Both of these statements are false, but true in their way. Maybe a better way of putting it is that for a long time, I tried to put my father out of my mind. He was no-go territory. Of course, he was there. In effigy. In all sorts of thoughts, feelings and in the things I did, in the people I liked and disliked. It was and wasn't 'him' in my mind. The effigy didn't come from nowhere. Things happened. He had been a violent presence in my early life. The trepidation of a Friday night. Late night rows downstairs. Fear. My mother bruised in the morning. Shame that everyone would 'know'.
>
> He left when I was 10. After that, I wasn't interested. Or so I thought. For many years, if asked when he left, I'd say, 'Oh, when I was 10 or 11 or 12.' It didn't matter. I actually didn't know for sure, as I was in a long-stay hospital at 10. When he left 'the family' I couldn't say. But I last saw him when I was 10. My memory is that he visited me in hospital. I have a photograph of him on the ward, in dappled sunlight, which has come to stand for this incident, but surely couldn't have been. On that occasion, so panicked was I that my mother would arrive, and there would be a scene on the ward that I begged him to go. I didn't see him again for 30 years.
>
> When I did, I had two fathers. I had the effigy. And this other, living, person. A person I'd sought out, at that point, when, after many years of therapy, curiosity outstripped fear and anger. When I could allow the only half-trusted, more benign memories I'd carried alongside the effigy some room: a sense memory of a steady presence, an intelligence. An image (a screen memory?) of a father sitting alongside me, giving me the cream off the top of the milk for my porridge, looking

with me out of the back window. What kinds of truth were these? Were they mere wishes?

I had long understood his marriage to my mother as dictated by the moralism of the times, she being pregnant. A forced union of two impossibly unsuited people. A pairing on a visit home, which proved a turning point in his life, ending his pre-existing relationship and the life he had escaped to across the Atlantic. A marriage that brought neither my father nor mother any happiness. Although the marriage was long over, the unhappiness remained.

My curiosity grew and I found I could allow it, with a no longer completely paralysing sense that to have anything to do with my father, to mention him, was betraying my mother. So, I looked for my father. The man I found was complicated (who would have guessed?). In his 70s, a man who had had a hard start in life. Whom life had made self-sufficient. Someone rather introverted, who needed his space. Who needed to read and go on long walks. Things I liked myself.

I had my questions – and accusations – for this father, and I had to think what to do with his answers. He denied some of what I remembered, evading responsibility, it seemed to me. He accepted some, too. So, then the question was for me: what was I going to do? What could I accept? My father's reply to my initial letter had arrived by return mail. Its eager openness surprised me. My curiosity met his wish for a reunion. We started from here.

It wasn't smooth going. The past was there and would rear up intensely. What was I doing? Yet, over the next 20 years and more, we built a new relationship. One of adults, which my father, never really cut out to be a father, was more able for. It was tentative and strange for a long time. That we were geographically distant helped.

It didn't mean forgetting the past, pretending bad things didn't happen. It was a kind of 'forgiving not forgetting, since injustices, hurts and fears reside "somewhere" in the heart, dormant or aroused'. Others might call this a generosity 'in the capacity to "give away" to another something that is good and worthy such as recognising a good aspect of the injuring other'. If so, I was the gainer too, in a process of 'repairing the damage to oneself caused by the other and by repairing the damaging "other" within oneself'.

The effigy faded away, mostly. Instead, I had neither no father nor two fathers. I had, for much of the time anyway (the dormant times) one father, who had done hurtful and selfish things to me and to others and who was also capable of kindness, who had his own story, who never expected anything but appreciated what came along. He was good and bad, in parts.

In his early 90s, my father had pneumonia and seemed to be dying. He recovered, to live several more years. But as he drifted in and out of mild delirium at his most unwell, his talk was of his mother, what a good person she was, what a good mother she was. Writing this, I find myself moved as I was then that this old man's mind, at this moment of illness, maybe dying, went to his mother, to something good that he'd carried inside himself all of his life. So here we have a moving and honest account of a father who was an internal fantasy, an object if you will, rooted in absence, and a 'father' who, while abandoning the role, could have a different kind of relationship with his adult daughter – they both changed, evolved, as did their relationship, into something, which could be internalised and managed, though in a different way that neither one of them had envisaged.

Anthony Joseph won the T. S. Eliot prize for his collection *Sonnets for Albert*, described as 'luminous' by the judges. 'From this strong field, our choice is *Sonnets for Albert*, a luminous collection which celebrates humanity in all its contradictions and breathes new life into this enduring form,' said Jean Sprackland, Chair of the judges. *Sonnets for Albert* is an autobiographical collection that weighs the impact of growing up with a largely absent father.

Reviewing the book in *The Guardian*, David Wheatley said that 'after much silence and absence in life', Joseph's father was 'painstakingly restored in death in a book-length "calypso sonnet" sequence'.

> But is there such a thing as an absent father? Here's Harry, where? In the Naughty Corner. And where's that? Well, it's just one corner of his mum's front room, cleared especially for him. He's there a lot. When he looks round, the other corners are all filled with things: books, the TV, a table with some papers on it: no angry black clouds floating out from this one corner, no screeching birds or thunder and lightning; it just looks like any other old corner. Except Harry is in it now, he's in it a lot. He sits, like his mother said he should when she shoved him there, and he thinks. He does think, but mainly he thinks about what he can next do to get right under her skin, even though he knows with one part of himself that this makes things worse, that she'll shout more, that he'll spend more time just sitting; and round and round it goes. Harry's head is down, his fingers run through his hair, he's not happy but in a way he's not unhappy either, this has now become part of life. Can anything stop this sad roundabout? So, what does he do to get put in this old corner? He says 'no' to everything, he throws things at her, he throws himself

down on the floor and does a sort of roly-poly all over the room ... he HATES homework, it takes hours to do, and mum just gets crosser and crosser. At school things are different, the teachers seem to know how to calm him down, he's good at helping other children who don't get the things in class that he gets – that makes him feel good. He does love his mum, but sometimes he hates her too, and he feels (and maybe he's right) that she hates him as well. And oh yes, let's not forget he wets himself, mainly at home, or at school when teachers forget to give him the 'go to the loo now' sign. He told mum he does know when he should go, but plain and simple he doesn't want to. What a pickle they are in. He wants a dad, you see. Mum hasn't given him one. He's very angry, but underneath he's very, very sad.

Here below is the account of another boy where no father was resident, and his two siblings had different absent fathers. What a complicated and difficult narrative.

A single parent story...

Darren's school was concerned about him, and had been for two years. He was withdrawn and had difficulty making relationships with both adults and peers. He would spend long periods rocking back and forth and sometimes putting his head down on the table, which the teachers saw as a means of escape. He appeared unhappy, anxious, possibly depressed and would not talk about how he felt either at home or at school. Communication, when at all, was surly and sometimes disruptive, and he had a slight hesitation in his speech. He did the minimal amount of work, though he was an able boy. There had also been episodes of stealing. The school had discussed this with his mother, but until that point, she had not acknowledged a problem. The three children in the family did not share a father, and there was no father resident. For a short time, the children's names had been on the child protection register because of grave concern about neglect: the family had been isolated at the time, and mother had been 'hard on the children'. Mother felt Darren was different from her other children; she did not know how to handle him and was reported at that time finally to be keen for help.

Neil had a slightly different but equally sad story. His mother had herself requested the referral because of his difficult behaviour during the last year. He had been disruptive and defiant both at school and at home. He denied there was a problem in either setting and said he was happy. His mother was a single parent, and Neil was the middle of three siblings. Neil's father did not visit, and he had not seen him for three years. Father had recently had a new baby in another relationship. Neil maintained that he saw his father 'quite often'.

As can be seen from these two referrals, both are middle children and have had somewhat different responses to their predicament. Darren has become withdrawn and out of contact, and clearly too in this family, there are concerns about mother's capacity to manage at a minimum accepted level. It might be seen that in this family Darren carries the inability to grieve for loss and move on: often hesitation in speech may be connected with things that cannot be spoken about, and Darren, like the three absent fathers, might be seen to represent issues mother herself found hard to handle. Neil is more openly destructive and unhappy but denies he has a difficulty. It does seem, however, that he knows something about his father, although father's new family may be a tortured piece of knowing for him. In the event, Darren's mother was not able to take up repeated offers of appointments (referral had been made by the school and the anxiety was clearly chiefly located there rather than in Darren's mother). Neil's mother, who had herself made the referral, was by contrast able to attend some family sessions and gained some insight into the meaning of Neil's behaviour, as well as some much-needed support for herself.

'The Child is father of the man' is a rather well-known line from William Wordsworth's poem:

> My heart leaps up when I behold
>   A Rainbow in the sky:
> So was it when my life began;
> So is it now I am a man;
> So be it when I shall grow old;
>   Or let me die!
> The Child is father of the man;
> And I could wish my days to be
>   bound each to each by natural piety.

This suggests that childhood experiences shape who we become as adults, emphasising the continuity of personality traits and characteristics from childhood to adulthood. It's a truism, but is it always true?

There are many inspiring stories of men who have succeeded despite the absence of their fathers, a hole in their lives that they have managed to fill. The absence of a father figure can present unique challenges, but these individuals have demonstrated resilience and determination to achieve their goals. Some notable examples include Barack Obama. The former President of the United States grew up with his mother and grandparents after his father left when he was two years old. His father, a Kenyan man from Nyang'oma Kogelo, died in 1982, having met Obama's mother in a Russian language class at the University of Hawaii. Obama says he still wonders about his absent father, and about how things would have been had his dad been there. 'I felt his absence. And I wonder what my life would have been like had he been a greater presence,' he said a day before one Father's Day. He called on other fathers to make spending time with their kids a priority even when times are tough. Despite the absence of his father, Obama went on to become a successful lawyer, professor, and eventually, of course, the president. So, he filled the hole left by an absent father, even though he thought a lot about him. The father is never absent. Can this family father wound ever be healed? If men don't have the support of their fathers, do they become disconnected from their authentic selves? Statistics tell us that more than 20 million children live in a home without the physical presence of a father, or someone who occupies that vital third point, and, yet, can there be a story of redemption and healing, for both the absent father and the son? The choices some men make result in personal happiness as well as making a better world for us all. There will be stresses present in every life: it remains our choice, whether it affects us deeply, or not. We all have struggles to overcome, and there are people who use these struggles to climb higher.

Steve Jobs, the co-founder of Apple, who died in 2011, was raised by his adoptive parents after his biological father, whom he never met, left him and his mother. His mother decided to give him up for adoption because of strong opposition from her own father who objected to the marriage to a Syrian. Weirdly enough, Jobs had eaten at his biological father's restaurant several times without knowing it, and his dad, who also did not know Jobs was his son, said, 'He was a sweet guy and a big tipper.' But Jobs' view was that, 'I learned a little bit about him, and didn't like what I learned'. So, his fantasy father had a greater hold on his expectations than the real live father of 'reality'. After his adoptive mother died in 1986, he eventually met up with his biological mother and his sister: 'she was not completely thrilled at first, but as we got to know each other, we became really good friends, as she is my family'. Despite his challenging upbringing, or perhaps in fact to rise above it, Jobs went on to revolutionise technology. He was a pioneer of the 1970s and 1980s personal computer revolution, alongside his early business partner Steve Wozniak. He was posthumously awarded the Presidential Medal of Freedom.

Another former US President, Bill Clinton was raised by his grandparents when his biological father was killed in a car accident three months before he was born. Another gaping hole. He overcame adversity to become a successful politician and leader. His grandparents instilled strong values into the boy, that everyone is equal, and no one should be treated differently because of skin colour. That was a lesson he never forgot. Later, he was reunited with his mother, now remarried (we do not know how this affected an adolescent boy), and they went to live in Hot Springs, Arkansas. Clinton as an adolescent shook the then president's hand, and decided he wished to make a difference in people's lives by becoming the president himself.

Nelson Mandela, the South African anti-apartheid revolutionary and president, lost his father when he was 9. He grew up under the care of other family members and went on to lead a nation and inspire the world with his activism. He wound up spending 27 years in prison for leading the African

National Congress, which strongly opposed apartheid policies that kept the Black population segregated. One can only assume he had strong relationships with his internal objects, and he had been old enough when his father died to internalise an abiding memory that carried him through such tough times.

O.J. Simpson, NFL star and actor acquitted of murdering his former wife and her friend, ran around, past and through defenders on the American football field. Born in San Francisco, he developed rickets and wore leg braces until he was 5. By this time, his parents, Eunice, who was a hospital administrator, and Jimmy, who was a janitor, had divorced, with Jimmy leaving the family home when OJ was four. OJ was raised by Eunice and ran a gang too. Later, OJ discovered his father was gay, but somehow these apparent difficulties served to make the boy rise above them, and even his rickets, which left him bow-legged, helped him to make quick cuts, sudden changes of direction, and speed out of them the other way. What a success – at least, on the football field. But one could wonder at his subsequent violence, whether as a result of discovering his father's true sexual orientation, or because of violence that had been visited on him early in life. When he was acquitted of murder, public reaction was divided along racial lines. While Black people were sure he had been framed, even sympathetic White people were convinced of his guilt. Be that as it may, 20 years later, he died, aged 76, of cancer.

These men's stories highlight how resilience, determination and support from other family members or mentors can play crucial roles in overcoming parental absence and achieving success. Each of them faced unique challenges, but they persevered, in spite of unconscious feelings of abandonment and loss, and left a lasting impact on the world. But where there is an absent father, a hole, if you will, some children do benefit from a strong therapist to help them overcome the unconscious loss, as the clinical material from my child and adolescent colleague suggests below.

My colleague, Sam Zuppardi, generously allowed me to include his clinical work: 'Changing the focus: towards the possibility of building new object relations with a male therapist, where there is an absent father'.

> I have been working with an 8-year-old boy who had learnt he needed to be extremely careful with a very unwell mum. He had no contact with his dad, had grown up alone with his mum and was hyper-attuned to her moods. He was adept at maintaining a neutrality that he believed would put no demands on her. In therapy I was initially treated as a very fragile object around whom the boy carefully oriented himself – fitting in so as to cause least disruption to my equilibrium. Interpreting this dynamic seemed to have no impact, and the result was that this boy made almost no impression on me in the early months of therapy. I found myself feeling bored and apathetic in what felt like increasingly repetitive, lifeless work. I was wondering whether it was going to be possible to continue the therapy. However, the boy began showing

me a new exercise regime: an extremely boring series of press-ups and sits-ups that I was supposed to watch him perform over and over. It was joyless and mechanical, and when I asked about the purpose of this routine, he told me he wanted to get some muscles and invited me to an arm-wrestle. I started to think about this invitation to wrestle and his newfound desire for more contact between us. Was he making an active bid for a relationship with me as a man/father/therapist figure with whom he could identify – someone who could be interested in the idea of us building up muscles together? I was able to respond in kind, becoming more active and offering him the metaphorical equivalent of an arm wrestle: something strong to push back against. This developed and our sessions took form around a series of lively symbolic battles, represented by maps drawn and scribbled on by both of us as we strove to destroy each other's armies. I noticed that the boy benefited from my active and playful presence: something that he could find in me to push against, and where his aggression could be met with a benign and robust response. He became enthusiastic, excited and antagonistic – in the best possible sense of the word. I was reminded of Anthony Storr's (1968) book, *Human Aggression*, which speaks up for that often misunderstood but vital life force. My patient had feared his own aggression towards a mother whom he imagined he might easily damage, but he was able to make use of me to explore a new and different kind of relationship. In doing so, both he, I and the therapy were brought back to life. While in this instance, we were able to find a fruitful space for a man/father/therapist within the work, another case comes to mind in which such a space and function were notably absent.

This was a 9-year-old girl I had been seeing for two years. She had an absent father and a deceased grandfather. There were no men in the immediate family system; the girl was raised by her mother and widowed grandmother. She was wary of coming to see a male therapist. The many complicated feelings she had about fathers – for which I was immediately a rich transference object – were largely defended against. I was kept under rigid control and not allowed my own mind or separate existence. Many sessions involved my following careful instructions, walking to routes my patient drew out on a map of the room (a very different kind of map to those of my previous patient) and being manipulated by a 'magic remote control' that dictated the speed and direction in which I moved. Moments throughout the two years when I resisted this control and asserted my own mind and separateness invariably led to tidal waves of fury, anxiety and confusion. The absence of a space where thinking together could be allowed was a very apparent deficit in the girl's emotional development. The idea of her letting go of her rigid control over me seemed terrifying for her. In one of our final sessions, the dolls' house had been set up with a family made entirely of children and women. Selecting the one male figure that was there, the grandfather, my patient systematically chopped his hair off and shredded his clothes before casting him aside. My comment that this seemed to be quite an attack was met blandly with the dismissive reply that it was 'actually a makeover', and I was ordered to follow instructions and play the part of one of the children in the house. Attempts to reintroduce some of the banished paternal function into the game (and the therapy itself) were met with unequivocal resistance. During this work, there were some hard-won moments of more benign connection between us that kept the therapy going, but it was exhausting work. The anxiety associated with allowing difference, particularly gendered difference and what that meant for my patient, was always pushing us backwards towards the established status quo. In the case examples above, my gender and how I was being related to were present and explicit in the work. There also seemed to be a fluidity in paternal and maternal function and the transference that co-existed irrespective of my gender. Gendered terms such as 'paternal function' or 'maternal transference' come with a huge amount of cultural baggage and historical context: centuries of sexual oppression and a stark power imbalance between the sexes (see *John Stuart Mill* again in Chapter 4 – JE). It feels important to acknowledge that a predominantly binary approach to gender means that using gendered terms, like 'paternal' for potency or 'maternal' for nurturing, without qualification, risks perpetuating unhelpful and reductive stereotypes about the function and value of both male and female characteristics, respectively.

Here is another example, taken from my own clinical caseload:

> Larry (not of course his real name) is king of the roost, the 8-year-old monarch. The only one, the only boy, whoopee! His dad left home when mum was pregnant, not wanting a child, but came back and fell in love; of course. Larry wanted to stay inside mum, but he came out eventually, big baby that he was, and took up his place in the family drama. Larry's king of the roost, he loves being filmed and acts up big time for the camera, but he's always very worried too, about a lot of things. Very, very worried. About dying, about getting old, about being lonely. Loud noises – oh, how he hates them! They make him jump, he runs and hides: the king of the roost turns all at once into the most frightened chick in the family. He wets his bed, right at the last minute before morning, as if it's hard to hold on to all that worry and wait till he gets up and gets to the loo. When his parents, who now expect their second baby in a couple of months' time, ask someone to see Larry to think about all his worries, he's a bit reluctant at first to come in, and then very reluctant to go. He tells the person (JE) about the worry bubbles in his tummy that make him feel so bad. He travels all the way to

France alone to see his grandparents, and he's proud of that. But there's something. Something that keeps that other side of him on high alert too. 'Do you know I have a little brother?', he asks. Little brother will not be born for another two months. Larry makes a set of things that are broken, even a tiny bit broken – the lizard whose tail is snapped off at the end, the toy with the wobbly leg – everything seems lost or broken, and Larry asks, 'Did they lose these things in real life?' Real life. In real life, a baby brother is on the way, and while parents think Larry may be like a 'third parent', it will be important to remember he is a little boy of 8 who will be supplanted by a baby and may be worried about how he really feels, underneath all the goodwill. Watch this space. Is there a catastrophe pending? Some thinking with his parents helped them understand how worried Larry gets, about things he can hardly verbalise, and his bed-wetting decreased and then gradually ceased.

Another case of individual treatment below from my caseload represents the predicament that may occur if a child comes from the 'single-parent family' constellation and has neither the support to overcome this situation, or the personality to 'rise above' it.

'Brian' was a boy who was conceived at a party who never knew his father. I have described previously (Edwards & Maltby, 1998) work done with an adolescent girl whose development was also compromised by the difficulties inherent for her in growing up without a father in the house. What these cases will show is the particular impact that their family situation had on each young person. As I emphasised earlier, being a child in a single-parent family is not a pathological condition, but can present a particular challenge to an individual, to which they will respond in a way determined by their individual psychological constitution and what they bring to their situation in terms of these factors. There will also be cultural issues to take into account, and it is vital to have a vertex that includes these where appropriate. In the case described below, referral was made following difficulties around school attendance, which could be seen as a symptom of a more profound difficulty to do with separation and individuation, and the lack of the third point to help with this. This along with another case was originally discussed from a different point of view in a chapter of a book about school refusal (Edwards & Daws, 1996).

'Thomas' had become increasingly school phobic as he approached secondary transfer and was referred to the clinic because of his nightmares and obsessive touching rituals. He had lived alone with his mother all his life, and she had been diagnosed as suffering from a serious illness soon after his birth. Thomas had been conceived while his mother was travelling around the world: his father was someone similarly circling the globe, and they interconnected briefly. Unlike Brian, however, Thomas did have somewhat of a relationship with his father, who was still travelling, but visited from time to time. The accounts I had via Thomas of his father was of a man who in his mid-40s seemed still to be living out his adolescent fantasies, with fast motorbikes and a disconnected itinerant lifestyle. Thomas's lifelong experience was therefore of a fragile mother without a father to help and support her. While consciously he seemed to have accepted his role of being merged with mother (with whom he was on first-name terms) in what could be described as a symbiotic union where they both even looked physically like two halves of one person, at an unconscious level, he was terrified of this merging. He showed this when for the first year of his once-weekly therapy, he played off-the-ground games and constructed dens in one corner of the room. I understood this as being in order to ward off contact with me as a frightening maternal object, projectively identified as being all-consuming, as Thomas himself also wished to intrude and take over. He spent sessions trying to play outside the therapy boundary by suspending objects over the window sill, attempting (and succeeding) in attracting the attention of other patients. It was clear that there was no notion of a boundary-keeper in his mind, no notion of a quiet reflective space. By getting rid in his mind of the idea of a father by taking his place, Thomas then himself feared takeover by a retaliatory and vengeful figure. It was difficult for Thomas to envisage a third position: he was either enmeshed or disengaged as a defence against this. For this child, the environmental difficulties of his infancy had prevented a working through of his ordinary omnipotence: his obsessive touching of boundaries could be seen as his own desperate attempt to contain himself.

Thomas asked me for 'miles of string', and he spent several sessions constructing elaborate webs in the room. He explained that he had made webs for as long as he could remember: that at first he made them in order not to get tangled up in them, but then he had 'given up'. He got into his therapy web and deliberately wound its threads around his limbs. An entangling union like that between himself and his mother was all that he could envisage. I saw this as a kind of symbiosis, though not as in the scientific terminology, where both parties gain by the relationship. He both invited and dreaded this union, and he had nightmares about it. Bowlby (1973) described a similar incident with a 9-year-old boy who wound himself up in the window cord, saying 'See, I'm in a spider's web, and I can't get out'. Thomas told me the story of Robocop, a man who had been made into a machine: 'He was hurt so badly he didn't ever want it to happen again.' I said perhaps he was also talking about a part of himself that it felt very risky to allow to make any contact with me. It was hard for him to imagine that we could be friendly without someone getting trapped or hurt. For Thomas, a container swiftly turned into a straitjacket. We talked about his heroes who were the macho stars of popular films. Thomas gradually began to be in touch with internal strengths that could develop once he had in therapy some experience of a relationship that could encompass dependency without overwhelming him. In the contained and consistent setting of the therapy room, he came to appreciate what could be called a paternal part of me that could both strengthen the maternal and protect it against his own powerful wishes to take over. Meanwhile, his mother received parallel support from a colleague. While initially she found it hard not to intrude into her son's therapy, over time, helped by the idea of myself and my colleague as a strong couple, she developed her own strengths and insights, as she unravelled the problematic relationship she had had with her own parents.

Thomas made secondary transfer amid concerns among us all about his capacities to survive it, but he managed and has continued to do so. His therapy ended, but his mother continued to have support in order to help Thomas with the vital separation on his way to adolescence. There were inevitably questions that arose again during our final sessions about whether I could let him go, and in the penultimate session, he announced that his wish-list for his birthday included a paint gun, goggles, camouflage, smoke grenades and a motor bike. I took this up in terms of his anxieties about me hanging onto him even though we had decided an ending date and were working towards it: would I let him go or would he have to put up a smokescreen, hit me and run? He was able subsequently to end on a note of sadness as well as hope, and what he took away was the knowledge that he could carry on his developmental path, without having to take care of his mother or be a premature adult. Again, triangular space for thinking provided new alignments, so that, with the idea of 'a notional couple', Thomas could be freed from the seductive web to achieve real growth.

In both these cases, individual work with the young person proceeded alongside individual work with the parents, both of whom, for their own internal reasons, had previously denied the importance of a two-person relationship in bringing up a child. It is this absence of a sense of the internal creative couple which is at issue here, since, as I have already indicated, there are indeed many instances when a parent can make internal space for their creative counterpart, and also provide external opportunities for vital identifications to be made. For these two lone mothers, there was offered the opportunity both to think with their own worker and thus develop a less isolated and falsely independent stance, and to perceive the two clinic workers as a strong couple, working together both for the development of the child and also in partnership with the adult part of the parent's personality in the service of the infantile needs of the young person. While this scenario is an ideal one, and in many clinic settings, there may well not be the opportunity for this parallel work to be offered, I think it is possible nevertheless to proceed, if the psychotherapist working with the child has a sense in her own mind of the strengthening presence of an other, a space for a father. In past years, the parallel work with a parent would have been carried out by psychiatric social workers. However, budget constraints and changes in the professional orientation of social workers have altered this picture, and child psychotherapists have had to think again about how to approach the question of work with a parent alongside the child's treatment. As the author points out, the intensive training in psychoanalytic work with children gives our profession a particularly rich base for this endeavour, and, in both these cases described above, it was the combined resource offered to the family that enabled the work to be done.

Another of my female contributors said:

When I was asked to write about relationships with fathers and the author asked me about mine, I said, "Well, I don't have one with him, we are estranged." She asked if I would write about it. I said I would, but it has proven to be more difficult than I thought it would be. (*As I have noted before, writing about something often results in the darkness echoing, and new thoughts emerging – JE*) I guess it is a bit complicated.

My parents were married when both were 18, and in fact (though it was never stated out loud), I am fairly sure it was my imminent arrival that had them 'elope'. My father was a high school dropout who joined the military as many young men looking for opportunity did in those times. |He is a brilliant man and performed so well on his GED (the test you take to achieve your high school degree when you quit school) testing that the USAF sent him to university where he obtained an engineering degree with honours and subsequently entered office training program, becoming a Lt. in the USAF and a pilot. He went on to fly during the Vietnam War as a forward air reconnaissance pilot, very dangerous work. The Air Force then paid for him to earn a graduate degree in aerospace engineering. He was an engineer on the B1 bomber program until late in his career when he decided to learn to fly fighter jets. He retired as a Major and went into the restaurant business with his brother.

My parents were far too young when they married, and quickly had two children: me and my younger sister 15 months later. They were ill-suited and married for lust not compatibility. My father was a working-class kid, extremely intelligent, but often in trouble. My mother was the only child of upper middle-class parents and very classically beautiful, but not my father's intellectual equal.

Their marriage was very volatile. My sister and I endured many angry arguments and a mother who was often anxious and depressed. We moved often as the Air Force moved my father to various assignments across the country.

My relationship with and feelings about my father are, as a result, complicated. As an adult, I have come to realise that even as a very young child, I went to great lengths to gain my father's approval, but I also felt protective of my mother in opposition to this. I can remember one vivid horrific fight between them when my father was threatening to leave us, packing his bags and pushing my mother away from the car such that she fell in the driveway. I was around 11 or 12. My little sister was crying and begging him not to leave, and I remember yelling at him to just go ahead and leave.

I look very much like my father. For a woman with a beautiful mother and beautiful sister, that is not a thing one wants to hear. But I have his intelligence. From a young age, I would have discussions with my father about politics and world events. Early in life, I adopted his worldview, which was an intelligent but conservative hawkish view common to military personnel during the Cold War. While I was very influenced by his views, I also felt very different about many topics and as I grew older and started to have my own thoughts. We had raging debates about topics such as civil rights, women's rights, and other social and political considerations of the time. These debates, as I entered my college years, became outright damaging to our relationship. He was always an extremely difficult person to please, very impatient, with a horrible temper.

He was a tennis player, so I learned to play tennis, or I tried to learn. He liked to sail and bought a boat, but when I tried to learn to sail, the outings would often end with him yelling at me for failing to do things right. He was an impatient teacher who yelled at me so embarrassingly during a doubles tennis match that the other players were mortified.

Yet I also admired my father, the brilliant Air Force pilot who would spend hours discussing world events with me. He also took me to baseball games when we lived in a major league baseball city. He could be charming and funny.

As I got older, I took on more responsibility for my mother's happiness. I can remember her crying when I left for college. Throughout her life, I never felt I could live too far away. When I was 26, my parents got divorced. While I felt that they should have divorced well before then, I was furious at my father for leaving my mother for a younger woman who was my age, a waitress who worked for him in the restaurant. I was fairly angry at my father, not for leaving my mother, I could understand that their marriage was very unhappy and they had really never been compatible, but because my father had always preached honesty and integrity to me. I felt he had been deceitful and hypocritical. He even had rules about his managers dating the staff. I had also always suspected he had cheated on my mother on other occasions.

My mother, who had never worked, was now alone and jobless at 44. I did not feel he was fair in the financial settlement. My mother did not handle the divorce well because she was fragile and abused and forced my sister and I to choose between them, to 'choose her side'. My father was actually willing to accept this arrangement.

He now had a new family, a wife with two young children, whom he adopted. My sister was more saddened by losing him and angry at my mother for forcing us to choose. I think I knew my mother was too fragile to accept us continuing to have a relationship with my father. Initially, I was ashamed by the estrangement, but honestly was also relieved. My father caused me great stress, and it was frankly easier for me to move on. I no longer had to suffer his judgment or failed attempts to gain his approval. I have only seen my father once since then, at my grandfather's funeral many years ago. My sister did attempt to have a relationship with him when my niece was born. She had much more difficulty with the estrangement. But he failed to come through, and she too gave up on a relationship with him.

I spent the rest of my mother's life helping her financially and trying to be there for her. More of the burden of caring for her fell to me, because my sister had young children. My mother was needy and difficult, but I have come to understand something I intuitively knew from a young age: she suffered from undiagnosed debilitating anxiety. She ended up suffering from Alzheimer's disease from the age of around 64 until she died in 2020 when she was 76.

For many years, I was embarrassed to tell people I don't have any contact with my father. My sister went to counselling with her minister about it, and he told her there is a difference between being a biological father and actually being a father to someone. He helped her to let go of her guilt. I no longer have any guilt. I have had many conversations over the years with friends who either have terrible relationships with a parent or are estranged.

I feel that I can say now, that sometimes people do not deserve to be in your life or that you have to choose the people, even if they are your parents, that you want in your life.

I do think I have been shaped in good and bad ways, as we all are, by both my parents. I know that many of my own challenging psychological and relationship issues stem from a childhood trying to please a very difficult-to-please father and trying to protect and make a mother happy who could not be happy.

My sister and I often talk about our sad childhood. We were certainly well cared for and not physically abused, but there was much anger and sadness in our house, which seeped its way into our own minds, as it is prone to do. My sister has gone overboard to ensure her children's happiness (as many of the parents of our generation have done). She did not want them to have the kind of childhood we had. But we both agree that this focus on ensuring your children are ALWAYS happy has perhaps not served them well. I, on the other hand, never wanted to have children. Perhaps subconsciously I just felt I would not be a very good parent. We were very fortunate to have grandparents we adored (my mother's parents) and who were great role models to us both in their loving relationship and who they were as human beings. They were very solid adults in our life, even though we only saw them a couple of times per year.

We have come to a place where we both feel that our difficult childhood did make us very resilient. We are both good human beings who have been successful in our careers and contribute to our communities. We also have come to an understanding that our parents probably did the best they could as people who had children when they themselves were only children. (*This realisation is crucial in the service of moving on – JE*) I look back on my life, I realise most people, even people with wonderful parents, faced challenges in those relationships. It is what you learn from those relationships, taking the good with the bad from them that helps you be a better person in your own relationships.

One of my contributors describes how he carried around a huge amount of anger towards an absent father, who left three little boys 'without a backward glance, or so it seemed'. His mother had found it difficult to cope, and this boy had been in and out of foster care, left with this huge rage inside his mind, which grew as he grew. He finally found out where his father was buried, and went to the grave 'to piss on it'. This he could not do, so he went back and started the engine of his car, to drive away as far as possible. But something made him open the car door and walk to the grave again. Maybe his father had walked away because he too felt unloved? This time his tears flowed, and flowed, and flowed. In that flood, he forgave his father, and felt as if a huge weight had been taken from his heart. While this may popularly be termed 'closure', for my contributor, it opened something up within him that had been rigidly locked off, and his creativity could flow again, in the space created by his father being 'the third point'.

I want to carry on by talking about a little girl who felt no need at all for fathers, or parents.

Once upon a time there was a little girl called Charlotte who lived in a Bubble with her (imagined) friend baby Sue. They had a lot of fun there: Baby Sue was great at making up all sorts of games – they played Hide and Seek, Jumping Up and Down till you fall over tired, Running around in circles screaming, Twirling round and round till they got so dizzy that they just laughed and laughed and laughed – and fell down all over again. It was all such fun. In Bubble Land, you didn't need to eat much, just drink Bubble Juice and let it fizz in your nose so you laughed a bit more. There was definitely NO SCHOOL. There was no crying, either, ever, until Baby Sue suddenly got cross about some little thing that didn't go her way and messed everything up, threw everything out of their little house in the bubble, and sat there with a VERY cross face until she and the little girl made friends again. They always did. It was such fun.

Meanwhile, not so very far away, just in another part of Charlotte's house, in fact, were her two parents. They too lived in a bubble, but a different sort of bubble, where they talked and dreamed of their lovely little fairy girl, and dressed her up in fairy clothes so she was the most beautiful little girl on the whole planet. (*Recall the 'too beautiful' pictures of children waiting to be adopted – JE*) She was also called Charlotte. Bubbles don't have doors usually, so it was hard for them to think they could get out of the bubble, and reach across to the other bubble where the two little people played and played, on their own, not needing parents or anyone to tell them what to do, what to wear, or how to be. I saw these parents for several sessions, but it was difficult indeed for them to think that their little girl needed help to escape her 'bubble'. As the late Irma Pick (2023) said, the therapist, while being empathically in touch with the part of the patient that needs rescuing, need also a 'paternal' figure to balance the situation and help the analyst remain on track.

Another of my clinical cases involved the boy with the twitch:

Once upon another time, there was a boy called Ferdinand who had a little twitch that sat on his shoulder. Twitch twitch, he would go, when anything upset him. Twitch twitch! When anything made him cross. When anything made him feel really really afraid. Well, then, the twitch got bigger and bigger, his whole body twitched and jerked, he'd stand on his head and wave his legs in the air: Look at me! Look at me! For goodness sake, just look at me! Twitch took over, he could shake his head and his eyes together, and he didn't have to think any more thoughts because standing on your head and waving your legs in the air is about as much as you can keep in your mind while you're asking your body to do such an unusual thing. So, all the frightened thoughts, the worried thoughts, the scary thoughts, just went over and huddled in a sad little heap in a lonely corner inside his head. They were NEARLY not there at all! Again, this boy was desperately trying to alert both his father and his mother to the worries that threatened to overwhelm him. We worked together as a team to understand this, and the possible meaning of the twitch.

And here's another clinical vignette about being a robot:

> What's the best thing about robots? We think of them as little machines we can tell what to do: then one day, they might turn round and tell US! They clink and they clank and they'll not ever get hurt, because they're machines, aren't they – not people like us with feelings. They just do what they want, don't feel anything at all, and have a good time: or do they? A little girl called Priscilla really wanted to be a robot, and sometimes, she turned herself into one. She was very proud of this: she could just switch her robot self off and on, and mostly, it was on, and then nobody could see what she was really feeling underneath. Feelings can be dangerous, best not to let them show. Clink clink, clank clank, I'm the best robot in the whole wide world!

> But, of course, robots don't smile, or laugh, or have much fun at all really – they just obey orders and get on with things in a very mechanical sort of way. Clink clink, clank clank. Here I come. But hey, what's going on here? Who's hiding behind all this clinking and clanking? Well, there IS a real girl there, who loves to play hide and seek, who loves to have fun, but just doesn't want to show anybody in case: in case what? Then something odd happens: the friendly robot turns out to be not so friendly, and takes over the whole show, or the no-show. Little hiding girl Priscilla isn't allowed out at all; the robot Priscilla keeps the door shut and it's only sometimes, and not very many sometimes, that the real little girl is allowed out. Well, she pretends she doesn't mind, that Robot can manage the show, but underneath, she does mind. She really minds. And when the real little girl is let out, all those feelings burst out – she gets terribly angry with her little brother, she wants to kill him. She gets terribly angry with her mummy and has to stay very near her just to be sure mum is OK, not killed off by Priscilla's murderous feelings, really, that Priscilla too is OK. What a muddle it all is! Feelings can be scary that's true, but can they be thought about and managed rather than being hidden away? Can the robot's power ever get smaller? Can the contact with the real Priscilla get stronger? Father was needed in this instance to help Priscilla be the real girl, not the robot who could 'never be hurt again', as she had felt so hurt by the birth of her brother, and not helped with these inevitable feelings.

Vincent's Volcano – the predicament of another little boy:

> Rumble rumble, louder and louder, then the volcano shoots fire up into the air, spitting bright sparks and then getting covered in that stuff called lava, which rolls fiery red down the volcano's sides, so get out of the way, please! You might end up dead, having inhaled poisonous fumes. But you might only be in the way if you're part of Vincent's family because I'm not sure I said that this is his own private volcano! Do you wish you had one? Well, maybe you do – but you may only see it when you're very very angry. It spits, yes it does, and children are NEVER allowed to spit though they may feel like it. They may feel like having a good hard spit, which then dribbles down somebody's face like the lava dribbles down the mountain. The volcano and the dragon that lives inside it chew up all the people, till there are just bones left, bare bones spat out and floating in the air, not sure whose bone is whose any longer Is that mum's thigh bone? Is that dad's skull? Is that Vincent's brother Matthew's two arms, now useless and bony, not anything left of him and of all the ways he can be actually quite kind to Vincent, even on his own birthday? And that is pretty scary, even though Vincent feels he is in charge. Maybe he's not? Then, of course, he does find it hard to go to sleep at night, it's nearly midnight and he's still awake, and you know what? Wait a minute – there's a DRAGON hiding under his bed, with dead children in his belly. It came out in his nightmares, and now, it's just hiding there, waiting. Is that the scary old dragon from the volcano? Vincent wants to be a doctor when he grows up, he wants to repair people. He wants to repair all those people who've been killed by the volcano, so he can have better dreams, and not be so scared of this dragon. But anyway, meanwhile he'll learn Kung fu and make scary dragon faces at anybody who annoys him. Then he'll grow up and marry his little girlfriend! Again, some working as a team with his parents helped make some sense of these spitting volcanic feelings, and Vincent could settle down to be less volcanic.

So, we have the idea of three-ness as being developmentally important, and this is the stuff of our work as child psychotherapists. How can this specifically be related to the 'two-ness' implied in the single-parent family structure? What happened to the third point? In 'The Myth of the One-Parent Family' (Johns, 1990), the author examines in some detail, the way in which myths embody our conscious and unconscious strivings, and our defensive manoeuvres to outwit the truth: 'the facts as they are'. He discusses Robert Graves's notion that the function of myth is to answer life's awkward questions about creation and death, and to justify existing social systems. As Robert Graves said, 'One constant rule of mythology is that whatever happens among the Gods reflects events on earth.' We make our gods in our own image rather than vice versa, and they emerge in order to structure and render meaningful psychic life. They enact our conflicts to do with envy, murderousness, guilt, and anxiety. Bion linked myths, and particularly the Oedipus myth, to the development of thinking itself. There never was yet, except in myth, a child born from one parent, and for every child born into this misleadingly labelled social structure, there will be presented the struggle to understand and overcome ordinary developmental omnipotence without perhaps the necessary external figures to help the giving up of an omnipotent stance. 'I created myself'.

Under the very label 'single parent' lie a host of family structures and family predicaments: from the family where father has never been known through degrees of 'lone parenthood' where fathers are not physically present but appear from time to time, or where divorce has institutionalised the family in terms of access orders and fixed rules of contact. In a sense, single parenthood as a concept can be seen as a continuum between these positions. No father in the house. As one young boy said to me, 'I haven't got a dad.' What impact does this have on children? How can this be managed, and what are the potentiating factors that can enable good enough developmental growth to occur?

Will a child without a father have an idea of what a father, or *his* father is, or is like? Is a father simply 'not mother'? Can a child get a true picture of his father through the eyes of his mother? (This is a particularly crucial question for boys, in terms of the need for identification.) I don't mean in any sense to indicate that a child in a single-parent family is doomed to struggle in vain and achieve partially or not at all the necessary integration of love, hate and ambivalence in order to achieve her or his best potential. What's clear is that many children within such a structure can and do achieve their potential, through the efforts of their remaining parent and by dint of drawing on their own constitutional capacities. Those fortunate enough to be born into extended and relatively close family structures can turn to alternative role models and feel supported to grow by drawing on the resources available to them. What is crucial is their own remaining parent's capacity to come to terms with their own story, and to offer coherence in potential adversity. The research of Fonagy et al. (1993) with the Adult Attachment Interview demonstrated that the crucial factor enabling parents to parent appropriately is the capacity to reflect on experience, however difficult, to find a meaning in it, and move on with a measure of resolution and forgiveness. In this way, experience can be integrated through thinking and metabolised fruitfully in order to provide a coherent framework for further development. What became clear when he and his colleagues interviewed mothers and fathers in the last three months of a first pregnancy, was that parents' stance in relation to their own history was predictive of the attachment status of their children at 12 and 18 months. Those individuals, both fathers and mothers, who were still hopelessly entangled in their past, or those who had become dismissive of early difficulty, were not able to provide a stable base for their children. So, we can see that it is not so much adversity that presents a stumbling block, but the way in which adversity is met and worked through. I'd like to suggest Arthur Schopenhauer's (1788–1860) maxim here: 'All truth passes through three stages: First, it is ridiculed. Second, it is violently opposed. Third, it is accepted as being self-evident.' Our present swarms with traces of our past, as Carlo Rovelli said.

Maria Rhode, Emeritus Professor of Child Psychotherapy at the Tavistock Clinic/University of East London, and an Associate of the British Psychoanalytical Society, works as Honorary Consultant Child Psychotherapist at the Tavistock Clinic, where she formerly co-convened the Autism Workshop. She has co-edited three books: *Psychotic States in Children* (Rhode, 1997) and *The Many Faces of Asperger's Syndrome* (Rhode, 2004), both Tavistock/Karnac, and *Invisible Boundaries: Psychosis and Autism in Children and Adolescents* (Rhode, 2006). She lectures widely nationally and internationally. Her recent articles include 'Asperger's Syndrome: A mixed picture' (Rhode, 2011a), 'The "autistic" level of the Oedipus Complex' (Rhode, 2011b) and 'Whose memories are they and where do they go? Problems surrounding internalisation in children on the autistic spectrum' (Rhode, 2012). Here, she expounds on the validity (or not) of the triangle.

> Emphasis might be on the way in which the vignettes concerning triadic situations might be linked to what I have more recently suggested could be thought of as the autistic level of the Oedipus complex (Rhode, 2011a; 2011b). Negotiating this involves coming to some sort of accommodation between the twin dangers of feeling obliterated by a physically seamlessly fused parental couple and feeling in danger of being engulfed when the third party is insufficiently present. (This particular danger has been highlighted in a first-person account by Ellen Stockdale-Wolfe (1993) in *Psychoanalytic Inquiry* entitled 'the Fear of Fusion'). The need for a third party (*the third point of the triangle – JE*) is apparent in all clinical material. It is also apparent in the familiar phenomenon that the material of children with autism may seem completely obscure during a session, but often becomes clear as soon as it has been written up: an act that introduces an element of distance and objectivity. This would place the understanding of Anthony's therapy within the theoretical context of Britton's triangular space and Rey's claustrophobic-agoraphobic dilemma. Alvarez' distinctive contribution in 'The sense of abundance' links to the importance of the mother's capacity to keep more than one thing or person in mind simultaneously: something that is particularly difficult for children with autism to credit.

> I would extend this argument to speculations about factors other than interpretation that may be important in bringing about change. Much has been written about this; what I particularly wish to focus on is that psychoanalytic work with children with autism has been a fertile source of new ideas, but that good therapeutic results have been achieved by

workers of differing theoretical persuasions (*what an important point that is, see* Psychoanalysis and Other Matters – *JE*), using a variety of frames of reference. This in itself implies that it is not insight alone that is the effective agent. I would propose that an important factor is the establishment of a triadic structure in which the interaction with the child links in the therapist's mind with a theoretical framework that is meaningful to her and engenders an intervention that is similarly meaningful to her. The child would then experience being someone whose nature and actions trigger a meaningful link with something previously present in the therapist, of which the intervention is the outcome, and this would be so, whatever the theoretical frame of reference. A number of instances exist in the literature in which the first establishment of a connection with a child on the autistic spectrum is made possible by the congruence of what the child brings with a personal, non-analytic interest of the therapist/analyst.

I'd like to end this chapter on single parents with a slice of clinical material, from my own caseload, about a boy whom I will call Brian.

Brian was referred to the clinic when he had stopped going to secondary school altogether in his first term after secondary transfer. He lived alone with his mother, who had previously suffered from an eating disorder, and Brian himself had been the product of a casual sexual encounter. His mother did not even know the surname of his father and had not seen him subsequently. At the time of referral, she had not seen this to be an issue of any importance. It was discovered in later work that Brian's mother herself had a history of difficult and inadequate parenting. Brian had managed to go to school in the relatively protected setting of a small primary school, but had found the task of emerging into the larger more un-contained environment of secondary school, where he was required to relate to many teachers during the day, and travel from room to room as well as subject to subject, in stark contrast to his memory of a nurturing primary experience with one teacher in one classroom, too difficult. If we relate this issue about separation back to the first crucial months in Brian's life with a depressed and unsupported mother, we could say that perhaps the primary task of separation had not been sufficiently negotiated in infancy, but this difficulty had remained latent until Brian was assailed by the impact of a large secondary school. He complained of headaches and stomach aches and stayed at home with his mother where they both slept a good deal of the time. As his absences from school were attributed to minor illnesses, it was almost a year before the severity of the problem was recognised. Brian was actually physically ill, but these illnesses were a symptom of his profound depression and despair. He had retreated into a hibernatory state with his mother, his primary object, and there was no father to offer him the energy to rouse himself from this lethargy, with which his mother unconsciously colluded because of her own unmet needs.

When we first met, Brian was silent in the presence of his mother but was more able to talk to me later on his own. He had some insight into the current predicament and said that he knew that he and his mother 'compounded each other's problems'. He also maintained firmly that he had 'never thought about' his father, and this remained his stance throughout the therapy that followed. Brian's defensive solution to his lack of a father was to refuse to acknowledge that there was a hole at all: a kind of annihilating denial that there had been two parents, even so fleetingly, at his conception. By the time the therapy began, Brian was in a special unit, and he seemed to be in the grip of depressive illness. During the assessment, his mother described staying up all night to ensure they made the morning times, because they both slept through alarms (and indeed it became clear that they had both ignored psychological alarms, which might have alerted them earlier before the situation became so problematic). Brian seemed to function on the surface in an apparently articulate way: a kind of 'second skin' solution (Bick, 1968), but beneath this skin lay a mass of fears to do with separation and abandonment should he give up his anxious position as feeder and provider for a depressed mother. By acting in a paternal way towards his mother, he usurped the father's role, but in so doing, he denied himself the opportunity to be angry about his loss, and this, I think, resulted in the draining away of his energy as he slept his life away.

In Brian's therapy, two themes stand out. He drew a house with a skeleton structure, which had no walls or roof, and I understood this both as the beginnings of something potentially stronger being built in his mind, but also an indication of an impoverished, semi-derelict internal world where he had been able to rely on no one. He found the idea of this internal exploration quite terrifying, although this latent feeling was usually masked by his accusations to me that he was bored and therapy was boring (while maintaining at the same time that he and his mother planned to buy a house on the road opposite the clinic). I think he managed to sustain his therapy in the early stages only because he incorporated it into his obsessive thinking about keeping to the same routes and routines. He described to me once how he had waited an hour in the snow for a bus that would take him by his usual route home, rather than catch another that would involve an adjustment in his route but get him home much earlier.

In the course of the last term of his three-term therapy, before he re-entered mainstream school, he made with great skill an anorak, which he brought to show me in its various stages. 'It's like a jacket, and not a disaster', he announced. I said I could see how proud he was to make something so difficult successfully, and not mess it up. He talked about the wadding that he would not use: it was to be a summer jacket (and we were approaching the summer break). 'The stripes from the inside go a different way, across and not down; it's not what you'd think', he said. I said I thought this jacket meant a lot to him, and that perhaps things too had changed quite a bit inside his mind, and he had been able to do better than he thought, like going back to school gradually. The jacket and its symbolic equivalent seemed to be an appropriate and necessary defence for a boy who had previously lacked hope. As Alvarez (1992) points out, a manic experience 'can signal the first glimmer of emergence from life-long clinical depression'. Brian began to be interested in the survival of the rain forests and the preservation of whales, who can communicate long distances under the sea. He began to connect, but in a covert way, with his anger, and drew space ships in which the guns were concealed under retractable flaps. His mother also saw a worker at the clinic, and it was through this partnership that she was able to connect with parental strengths and make a separation between her own needs and Brian's needs. She made a new sexual relationship and started part-time work.

Brian ended his therapy abruptly, following a lively and angry session shortly after an apparently successful re-entry into school. He said I had never been any use, and I had never answered any of his questions. I had no recollection that he had ever asked me any. I think in the transference, I became the absent father who had not been there to answer his questions about growing up. He left me rather than be left himself, and while this is only a partial solution, it gave him the strength and energy to return to school.

References

Alvarez, A. (1992). *Live company: Psychoanalytic psychotherapy with autistic, borderline, deprived and abused children*. Routledge.

Bick, E. (1968). The experience of the skin in early object-relations. *International Journal of Psychoanalysis*, 49(2–3), 484–486.

Bowlby, J. (1973). *Attachment and loss. Vol. 2: Separation: Anxiety and anger*. Basic Books.

Edwards, J., & Maltby, J. (1998). Holding the child in mind: Work with parents and families in a consultation service. *Journal of Child Psychotherapy*, 24(1), 109–133.

Fonagy, P., Steele, M., Moran, G., Steele, H., & Higgitt, A. (1993). Measuring the ghost in the nursery: An empirical study of the relation between parents' mental representations of childhood experiences and their infants' security of attachment. *Journal of the American Psychoanalytic Association*, 41(4), 957–989.

Johns, M. (1990). The myth of the one parent family.

Pick, I. (2023). *Authenticity in the analytic encounter*. Routledge.

Rhode, M. (1997). *Psychotic states in children*. Routledge.

Rhode, M. (2004). *The many faces of Asperger's syndrome*. Routledge.
Rhode, M. (2006). *Invisible boundaries: Psychosis and autism in children and adolescents*. EFPP/Karnac.
Rhode, M. (2011a). Asperger's syndrome: A mixed picture. *Psychoanalytic Inquiry, 31*(3), 288–302.
Rhode, M. (2011b). The 'autistic' level of the Oedipus complex. *Psychoanalytic Psychotherapy. 25*(3), 262–276.
Rhode, M. (2012). Whose memories are they and where do they go? Problems surrounding internalization in children on the autistic spectrum. *International Journal of Psychoanalysis, 93*(2), 355–376.
Stockdale-Wolfe, E. (1993). Fear of fusion: Nonverbal behavior in secondary autism. *Psychoanalytic Inquiry, 13*(1), 9–33.
Storr, A. (1968). *Human aggression*. Atheneum.

8 Fatherland

The Elephant in the Room

It was not possible for me to follow up the book *Grandmotherland* (Edwards, 2024) with a book called *Fatherland*, because of its deadly and unfortunate associations in the twentieth century. This was indeed 'the elephant in the room', so very large, leaving little space for other thoughts. In English, the word 'fatherland' was first recorded in the 1200s, possibly influenced by the Latin 'patria'. The ancient Greek *patris*, fatherland, led to *patrios*, of our fathers, thence to the Latin *patriota*, and the Old French *patriote*, meaning compatriot. The Welsh national anthem begins 'Land of my Fathers'. Other groups that refer to their native country as a 'fatherland' include the Armenians, the Estonians and the Finns. The concept of 'fatherland' or 'Vaterland' in German was central to Hitler's ideology, as is well known. For him, it represented a mythical and romanticised notion of the German nation, deeply rooted in nationalist sentiments and racial purity. Hitler's vision of the fatherland was one of militarism, expansionism and the dominance of the Aryan race. He exploited this concept to manipulate and mobilise the German people, ultimately leading to the atrocities of the Second World War and the Holocaust. The Nazis developed their ideology based on racism and the concept of *Lebensraum*, 'living space', and they had seized power in early 1933. In 1941 or early 1942, it was decided to murder all the Jews in Europe. They were deported by rail to extermination camps. If they survived the journey, they were then killed with poison gas or employed in forced labour camps where many died from starvation and abuse or were used as test subjects in deadly medical experiments. A few Holocaust perpetrators faced criminal trials; billions of pounds were paid in reparation, though of course falling sadly short of their losses. The Holocaust has become central to our Western consciousness as a symbol of the ultimate in human evil. Six million Jews were murdered, as well as 1.8 million Poles, 270,000 disabled people, 500,000 Romany people and 15,000 homosexuals. The murders were carried out primarily by mass shootings and poison gas in extermination camps, chiefly Auschwitz, Birkenau, Treblinka, Belzec and Sobibor, as well as Chelmno in occupied Poland.

And what of Hitler's history with his own father? While the Holocaust can in no way be excused or explained by thinking of Hitler's early life, the fact is that his early history was difficult and devastating. He was beaten many times by his father, Alois Hitler, a customs officer (born Alois Schicklgruber) often to the point of unconsciousness, once till he was in a coma, and the son vowed never to show his pain. While it might be all too easy to point to Hitler's own disavowed pain being projected forward, one might understand that this could be just one factor in the terrible inhumane consequences that followed as Hitler became an adult. Young Adolf once proudly told his mother that Alois hit him 32 times and he hadn't cried. I guess we all have to find pride in our accomplishments somehow.

There's an anecdote attributed to Alois Jr (more recently Adolf), which you can go back to when explaining the severity of the abuse within Hitler's household. When the boy skipped school to build a toy boat, his father whipped him until he lost consciousness.

It was only after Alois Jr successfully ran away a few months later that Hitler became the primary target. Hitler was a particularly stubborn child, used to getting his way. Alois Sr was a man hardened by decades of pulling himself up by his bootstraps. Putting them together produced a catastrophic battle of wills. Young Adolf regularly received thrashings. The more he cried, the harder his father seemed to hit, and after reading about a superhero, Karl May, Hitler resolved never to cry out when he was beaten. It's unclear how true this is. What we do know is that this iron-will mindset would remain with Hitler until his death.

This chapter appears quite late on in this book, in order to indicate its relevance, but in relative terms. Currently, both Russia and Ukraine talk of defending the Fatherland, and Norway and Denmark also refer to the Fatherland. The younger generation of German people learn that while there is no way of denying the past (their grandparents might have been part of the events of the Second World War and may have silently tolerated the atrocities), they are less overwhelmed by past events, even though political parties like the National Democratic Party of Germany have openly praised Hitler and propounded a racist stance. This increased support for far-right groups makes the situation, despite thoroughly documented facts, complex and complicated. The British revisionist historian and Nazi apologist David Irving was sentenced to three years in prison after he admitted denying the Holocaust.

An eight-member jury at a court in Vienna convicted Irving, 68, a few hours after it began its deliberations on the first day of his trial. Irving then told the court he had revised his opinion after seeing the personal files of Adolf Eichmann. Speaking in German, he told the court he now accepted that the Nazis had killed millions of Jews. This drama was speakingly enacted in the (2016) film *Denial*, directed by Mick Jackson and written by David Hare, with Timothy Spall playing the part of Irving.

There are no easy answers, but we need to keep the questions rolling. Who was Hitler's own father, and did Hitler himself have Jewish ancestry he wished to expunge?

In 1931, Adolf Hitler ordered an investigation into the rumours regarding his ancestry, and they found no evidence of any Jewish ancestors. After the

Nuremberg Laws came into effect in Nazi Germany, Hitler ordered the genealogist Rudolf Koppensteiner (1937) to publish a large illustrated genealogical tree showing his ancestry. This was published in the book *Die Ahnentafel des Führers* ('The Pedigree of the Leader') in 1937 and purported to show that Hitler's family were all Austrian Germans with no Jewish ancestry and that Hitler had an unblemished 'Aryan' pedigree.

Following the war, Adolf Hitler's former lawyer, Hans Frank, claimed that Hitler told him in 1930 that one of his relatives was trying to blackmail him by threatening to reveal his alleged Jewish ancestry. Hitler asked Frank to find out the facts. Frank says he determined that at the time Maria Schicklgruber gave birth to Alois, she was working as a household cook in the town of Graz, that her employers were a Jewish family named Frankenberger and that her child might have been conceived out of wedlock with the family's 19-year-old son, Leopold Frankenberger. 'Might' is the word here.

Back in those days, hitting your wife or child was far more acceptable. Women often relied on their husband's income, and for all his flaws, Alois Sr did make sure his family was financially taken care of. It was a horrible situation, but the truth of it is, it could have been worse. But this does not negate the physical and psychological damage he wrought on the family. They simply didn't appear to have a feasible exit route – except if Alois Sr were to suddenly die. Which, incidentally, he did on the 3 January 1903.

German people born well after the terrible events of the Holocaust are understandably ambivalent. As one of my contributors said:

> Any group of humans that needs to exterminate another on some spurious pretext is not in my good books, but it is starting to get boring when the younger generation is constantly reminded of what their ancestors have done. A bit like the British in India or the Opium Wars in China. How do you feel about that?

In Bob Dylan's (1964) album, 'The times they are a-changing', there are lines that sum up a rolling situation: 'Germans now too had God on their side.' Barbarism tends always to come clothed in moral righteousness.

References

Dylan, B. (1964). *The times they are a-changing* [Album]. Columbia Records.
Edwards, J. (2024). *Grandmotherland: Exploring the myths and realities*. Karnac.

9 Being the Father to Our Own Stories
Seeing and Being Seen

I was fascinated by the different stories that were told about the sculptor Antony Gormley's figures that were placed on high buildings around the South Bank in London. This 'Event Horizon' exhibition seemed to me, among many other aspects, to tell the story of fathers seen from a distance, and considered (as the jacket of this book portrays). So, with the permission of the people who attended the exhibition, I recorded the sentiments that were expressed:

One disabled woman, confined to a wheelchair, unable to move, said: 'You'd get such a wonderful view!'

Another thought from a nearby man: 'I feel there's, if you like, an unspoken bond between them and me – it's a celebration, touching the transcendental without having to say anything, a bit like being understood without words.'

Second woman said: 'I stroked the ones in the gallery, I would probably do that up there, it's a friendly experience. (*Perhaps a parental experience? – JE*) I felt very close to the figures inside when I touched them. I'd touch them but not talk, they don't speak, they're "completely apart" – there would be a kind of wordless communion.'

Her female friend agreed, but with rather strong reservations: 'Yes they are "something apart" – but they don't come across to me as being tender or loving, they are very cold.' (*Perhaps her view of her own father? – JE*)

First woman: 'Not to me, I feel very close to them.'

Man: 'I think they are very private people, I wouldn't intrude in on them unless they made the first moves. (*JE apologises here for her intrusion!*) They add a marvellous presence and give a spiritual dimension which is totally lacking in the city at the moment, which is about mammon and making money – we need to present another facet and they do that, they

DOI: 10.4324/9781003521846-10

add to human experience, the human condition. Yes, I will miss them when they are taken away.'

First woman: 'Also it's good watching people watching them, looking for them (*as with looking for father coming home from work as the Magritte painting depicted – JE*), it gives you a whole different dimension.'

Another man and a woman sitting nearby were also very interested to have a conversation about their experiences of the figures.

The woman began: 'It certainly gives us something to look at – makes you feel different about distances, it's not just blocks then, there's more a feeling of being scaled. It's quite odd really – in a way, a bit spooky, thinking of men walking across roofs, a bit like the exhibition and the white-out space, a sudden appearance like that is a sudden disappearance – it sort of makes you feel you have been put down to scale yourself, you are another little figure in a bigger landscape, makes me feel part of the landscape myself. (*Here, we have an example of seeing oneself in the third position – the Oedipus complex… – JE*)

Her companion continued: 'It's so interesting, a human form on top of a building, turning it upside down in a way, the buildings usually dominate people. It raised issues about how you display sculpture and where do you put public art – on a plinth? In a gallery? Or places that kind of surprise and shock? I know there was concern about suicide when they first went up, maybe people still think that – they are on top; I'm not up there with them.'

The other woman agreed: 'Yes, in my scale I am definitely down here.'

The man went on: 'There's the repetition of the figures too. They are not straightforwardly representing or doing anything, their features are smoothed off; they're anyone, Everyman in a way – what is the action they are engaged in? It is surveillance, are we being watched by these brooding figures, which is how they can come across sometimes if you catch them at certain angles – they are far from standard, although they are all the same – their location in different places gives different meanings.'

His companion said: 'I hadn't seen them as ominous, although having said that, you could also say they are slightly spooky, but also playful, and unexpected (*as fathers can show different aspects of themselves – JE*) – a great contrast to blocks of functional architecture – the architecture can have an overwhelming quality and they reduce that feeling (*as a father can give his child a sense of being themselves in the world – JE*), give you more a sense of fun – cocking a snook at architect's seriousness (*perhaps the father's innate sense of being 'right' – JE*); the blockiness of it, figures on the tops of the building are disarming, you can have a sense like a child of leaping from roof to roof.'

Man: 'They are unexpected, that's so good, it makes you pause, because there's a sort of disjunction, they make you look at the world slightly differently, gives a different sense of scale. The Angel of the North is so vast and then he's also done very small figures in Field, these are human size, not massive or tiny.'

Woman: 'They really open up the space; we don't normally think of the tops of buildings and the sky above them, they make you look up at the sky. There are so many figures of women everywhere, why not see a naked man? That's fine.'

Her companion suggested: 'I think it would have a different meaning because there are different associations to a woman's body – maybe people would say quite different things. As a woman, you'd probably feel vulnerable if you saw a naked woman up there, it might be a bit dodgy. They don't make me feel vulnerable as a man, but you couldn't get away from all the usual associations with women's bodies in art; it's quite good to see the male body in a position of vulnerability. It doesn't feel abusive in the same way as it might if it were a woman's body; it would feel abusive then, I think. It's tempting to say to them "Jump!" – they look like the suspended figures inside who are falling.'

The woman disagreed: 'Oh no, I'd say carry on looking up! I don't think they can see us. For me, they are in their own space, in a different plane.' (*How distant is one's father? – JE*)

The man looked very thoughtful, and then said slowly: 'There's something interesting about their posture, reminds me of diving when I was a child; you have your hands straight down and then you lift up on your toes (he stands up with some energy and does it) – I think that posture of theirs is almost like that, something to do with high diving – there is that same element of waiting, stillness and concentration.'

The woman agreed: 'Yes, they should stay longer but not for ever, because you don't want to lose that element of surprise, surprising something in all of us.' (*Fathers age, become grandfathers – JE*)

The man suggested: 'They could be moved around – you could have a year, say, not having them, then they could appear in different places. They've got a meaning much beyond most public sculpture.'

> The woman ended: 'It's that thing about London, it's so great to have these amazing things happen, how lovely for our city to have these surprising things!'

Finally, I talked to a young woman with two children, while the children were taken off along the embankment by their grandfather.

> They seem like such still figures in this big city landscape to me. I think of them observing time and movement, not threatening – a bit like the tide going in and out – you stop for a second to go where they are in your mind, you hold and let everything else continue round you, be at peace and at one with them, in unmeasured time – not physically but spiritually up there, because they are at one with the concrete environment, being made of industrial materials, they're part of the nature of the city, in a way, there are particles that cling to them all, like barnacles, they wouldn't say anything, they just are. You could go alongside them and then embrace that space and time, be as unintrusive as possible, a bit like the cloud cube, become part of it without interrupting them, join them and then come away again, a sort of fluid connection – you might have a conversation with them emotionally, and see what they see, the people, the buildings, the environment, what's behind you, what's in front of you. I've seen Gormley's work before in different places – maybe we might have something else up there? I think of them as sort of spiritual mentors – they're not looking at us but up at the sky, and we look up at them and get something from that.
>
> Another young man I interviewed said: 'We're all looking for something.'

As I hope the spread of conversations above indicates in different ways, this search, while diverse, seems also to group around different ideas related, as I suggest, to unconscious processes: wishes, desires and anxieties, perhaps about the father or father substitute. The statues, one might hypothesise, inhabit for the beholder what Winnicott (1971) called 'the transitional space'. This was originally conceived of as developing a space between mother and infant during the process of separation and individuation, where the 'transitional object' appears, what he called 'the first non-me object' (*the father or third – JE*), to aid in the onward journey with the issues to do with separation, loss and mourning (*as well too as issues of gain, when the infant turns towards the wider world – JE*). This space evolves with maturity into the space where adults play, and creativity, may grow and elaborate into cultural and aesthetic experience:

> I have used the term cultural experience as an extension of the idea of transitional phenomena and of play, without being certain that I can define the word 'culture'. The accent indeed is on experience. In using

the word culture, I am thinking of the inherited tradition. I am thinking of something that is in the common pool of humanity, into which individuals and groups of people may contribute, and from which we may all draw if we have somewhere to put what we may find ... cultural experience begins with creative living first manifested in play.

(Winnicott, 1971, p. 116)

So, in other words, the child is indeed, to quote Wordsworth once again, in this sense, father to the man.

While some of those I spoke to saw the figures as benign, benevolent, superego figures of an almost advisory kind ('spiritual mentors'), for others, specifically the two adolescent boys, they had a more threatening mien. One could think of ways in which their very developmental stage had awakened for these adolescent boys earlier images of a father who protects mother from the infant's desires, and who could be seen in a castrating and potentially threatening way, as a reversal or projection of the boys' own impulses and wishes (see Freud and Klein for an elaboration of thinking about the Oedipus complex, its stage of development for working through, and the timing of its inception in the mind of the infant or young child). It was notable that only one (woman) interviewee felt that the figures were remote and cold: perhaps in identification with critical superegos such as Klein described (Klein, 1963, p. 255). In terms of the male/female issue, predominantly one could suggest that the male statues were seen as wise (except in the cases of the adolescent boys, who saw them as threatening) paternal figures. The notion of female figures gave rise to thoughts of women in their sexual rather than maternal role (and the related issue of feminism), although one woman talked of the statues inside the gallery she had stroked 'in wordless communication', which could be seen to be connected to infantile memories of a preverbal communion with mother; what one might term an intimate maternal space. The last interviewee, when she talked of qualities of hardness and softness, seemed perhaps also in touch with this aspect. This was also alluded to, but more tangentially, by those who talked of architecture being 'humanised' by the appearance of the figures: as it were benign parental figures who help the child make sense of the world. In other ways too, there seemed to be a thread of thinking very much in touch with the experience of being a child: running, diving, watching the boats come in to the harbour and, as a grandparent, showing grandchildren something of the world around, which is exciting and full of potential: a sense of celebration of life and potency, aspiration rather than omnipotence. The joy and re-realisation with which the man described his diving child-self seemed a clear link with the theme of potential and exploration. Gaston Bachelard quotes the travel writer Philippe Diolé: 'in deep water ... the diver to loosen the ordinary ties of time and space and make life resemble an obscure, inner poem' (1969, p. 206). It made me recall in retrospect a patient of mine, a rather depressed boy who defended against feelings by acting out; this behaviour had caused him to be excluded from two schools. When he made (for the first time, successfully) a paper aeroplane, instead of interpreting that he wanted to fly away from his worries, I suggested that he also had a sincere wish to fly in a freer way, to feel less ground down by a history of failure. He looked at me intently and asked, 'Did it take you a long time to train for your job?', which I took to be his appreciation of the way I could acknowledge both his previous despair and the potential emergence of some hope. Both flying and diving in these contexts refer to hope rather than despair. The issue of the statues remaining in their places or being taken away provoked different responses, which seemed in some cases to be connected to the idea that they represented 'spiritual mentors' offering a needed containing potential, the desire of the individual to be held in mind: parental figures holding children (or the infantile aspects of the self) by their gaze, which was described by one man as 'mesmerising'. Other people interviewed, while clearly having a sense of their powerful presences, seemed more willing to accept the idea of their being taken away, but perhaps replaced later with something different. Referring back to Freud's conversation with his 'two young friends', the notion of being small and transient in relation to a larger and perhaps unfeeling universe seemed to hover around the edges of some conversations. Of course, these short interviews could only touch on some of these aspects rather than explore them in depth. However, the thanks I received from many of my interviewees led me to hope that more thoughts might be generated later.

At the end of her life, Melanie Klein wrote a paper 'On the Sense of Loneliness', published posthumously (1963). She talked about the perpetual human wish for 'an understanding without words'. One of my interviewees previously quoted had expressed the same thought. Klein went on to say, 'Full and permanent integration is never possible, for some polarity between the life and death instincts always persists and remains the deepest source of conflict.'

The longing to understand oneself is bound up with the need to be understood by the internalised good object – that is, perhaps the father. It seemed evident to me in the course of these interviews that the real and often deep responses to Gormley's statues over the city is a mark of this longing, present in us all, at an unconscious level: a longing that may be 'surprised' by works of art, or 'the trap', which Gormley himself referred to, which give us, to requote Winnicott, 'somewhere to put what we may find'.

In September 2007, the *Guardian* published a letter from a reader wondering if others also felt bereft at the absence of the 'Event Horizon' figures, after they had been taken down. She talked about there being something 'magnificent and comforting' about their presence, ending with 'they certainly fulfilled a very important function: they persuaded complete strangers to strike up conversations about art'. Perhaps, or so I like to think, she was one of the people who was generous enough to talk to me about the figures and what they might mean to the individual. What was hugely interesting to me in these conversations was the way in which so many layers of meaning were revealed, some of which I have touched on here, but re-reading the interviews seem to indicate to me more lines of discovery that I might have pursued, in terms of social and cultural studies, given a different perspective from that offered by my own professional training and interests.

Sculpture in the twenty-first century is now very rarely commemorative of 'great figures' and is beginning to be increasingly recognised as being able to give some sort of identity to public spaces, what might be called a human dimension. The vast and impersonal spaces created by London's city architecture around the South Bank were for a short while given a human dimension by Gormley's figures, and his title 'Event Horizon' resonates with this idea of ourselves as individuals perched on the edge of a vast space, internal as well as external, where different solutions may be posed and meanings sought, about fathers and a sense of personal identity. When President John F. Kennedy opened the Robert Frost Library in Amherst, Massachusetts, in 1963, he sent out a resounding challenge and rationale for the presence of art in our world:

> The artist, however faithful to his personal vision of reality, becomes the last champion of the individual mind and sensibility against an intrusive society and an officious state ... I see little of more importance to the future of society and civilisation than full recognition of the place of the artist. If art is to nourish the roots of our culture, society must set the artist free to follow his vision wherever it takes him.

I submit that these short interviews do indeed attest to the artists being able to tap into truths about our nature, and that the meaning of Gormley's work lies in a very real sense in the eye of the beholder, with his or her internal preoccupations about flying and falling, seeing and being seen, in the ongoing and fundamental dialectic of the container and the contained.

The drive towards narrative exists in us all, as we strive for meaning in what is (what a cliché now) called, 'the journey of life'. There is a seemingly irresistible drive towards making a narrative that fits your recollections, such as they are. As the late, great, Nobel Prize-winning short story writer Alice Munro said about narratives of the self:

> Memory is the way we keep telling ourselves our stories – and telling other people a somewhat different version of our stories. We can hardly manage our lives without a powerful ongoing narrative. And underneath all these edited, inspired, self-serving stories there is, we suppose, some big bulging awful mysterious entity called THE TRUTH, which our fictional stories are supposed to be poking at and grabbing pieces of. What would be more interesting as a life's occupation? One of the ways we do this, I think, is by trying to look at what memory does (different tricks at different stages of our lives) and at the way people's different memories deal with the (same) shared experience.
>
> (Munro, 2010)

Everybody's doing their own novel of their own lives. ... and we end up with a very discontinuous, discordant, very contemporary kind of novel. I think what happens to a lot of us in middle age is that we can't really hang on to our fictions any more.

(Rothstein, 1986)

If you were adopted, what is the tale you tell yourself about your birth father? Then of course there is the freedom of forgetting. Ah, narrative, which can change between each teller... Every person's life is a rich narrative, filled with unique characters, engaging conflicts and defining climaxes. More than just a sequence of events, our life stories are profound reflections of our innermost needs, desires and aspirations. These stories shape who we are and who we aspire to become, offering us insights into our own personalities and the collective human experience. How can we understand the narratives of our lives?

Life, in its essence, can be seen as a series of chapters, each narrated with its own set of challenges and triumphs. These personal narratives do more than simply recount what happens to us; they mirror our deepest ambitions, fears and joys, revealing more about our inner selves than we often realise.

The characters, the people who enter our lives, family, friends and rivals play significant roles in our personal growth and are often reflections of ourselves.

Is this a self-portrait with words? Yes, it seems to me that a person ought to be able to tell the story of himself, like Rousseau did. 'And I have suddenly a desire to search my soul, to search it in holy earnest ... my guiding principle here will be the truth!' (Cusk, 2011, p. 73).

Hmm, whose truth? This gem of an idea started with the writer, critic, poet and personal friend, the late Al Alvarez, who remarked when asked about his memories of Sylvia Plath: 'I've more or less forgotten about it'—so can we move from acceptance to forgiving to forgetting without splitting, or repression, but as a healthy move forward into a world where we are not encumbered by grievances or sadnesses over things past which can then trammel the present and compromise the future? (That is, to parallel with Fonagy's research 'Free' as opposed to 'anxious, ambivalent and entangled', leaving no space for the emotional cues of a child OR of future developments in the self?) Is there something in the onset of Alzheimer's that actually mirrors a state that might be helpful for us all, rather than something to be feared? Is nostalgia the answer? Can we embrace the freedom of forgetting?

'Nostalgia' was a term first coined by a Swiss doctor, Johannes Hofer, in a dissertation submitted to Basel University in 1688. It was meant to be used as a medical term to describe a depressed mood caused by intense longing to return home – coming from the Greek word *nostos*, the longing for home as portrayed by epic heroes such as Ulysses. But no *nostos* can change the fact that there can never be 'a return to the same'. In a book called *The Future of Nostalgia* (Boym, 2002), the author makes a distinction between 'restorative' nostalgia and 'reflective' nostalgia. Nostalgia of the restorative kind concentrates on the *nostos*: returning to the lost home; reflective nostalgia, on the other hand, concentrates on the *algos* – the longing and the sense of loss – what Klein (1963) called 'pining'.

Sohn (1983) wrote a paper on nostalgia in which he attempted to differentiate between what he termed 'true' and 'false' nostalgia. I recall when I presented a paper at a conference on the film *Nostalgia*, someone afterwards said, 'most people were in tears'. These struggles around loss and change, mourning or melancholia, affect us all, and we need beacons to guide us.

Central to this issue of nostalgia and the sense of loss is the notion of time. Freud (1912–1913) noted that the unconscious is timeless. Jacques (1982) reminds us of the need to discriminate between 'objective' and 'subjective' time: the first is marked by measured uniformity of linear intervals, while the latter is irregular, dependent on multiple psychological factors. Linked to this is the notion of the impersonality of time, neither cruel nor kind, which carries us inexorably from birth to death. In a timeless realm, by contrast, one is locked into a frozen state outside time, with no hope of change or growth, a kind of existential depression that also locks the person so gripped into endless repetition compulsions. The subject is chained to traumatic events, which cannot be psychologically represented (re-presented), in a way which facilitates moving on. The dominance of these conscious as well as unconscious thoughts then reduces or completely negates the capacity for new emotional investments that might enrich the inevitable passage of time.

An adolescent patient came to me with a psychiatric diagnosis of 'post-autistic'. He had indeed emerged already from a profoundly autistic infantile state, after a traumatic birth and difficult early life, through some previous analytic work undertaken when he was in the latency stage. He continued to make progress. Whether or not one considers that autism can be successfully treated with psychoanalytic work (and there are, of course, differing views on this), this young man did eventually live independently, which was an outcome his parents had never dared hope for. Through the work we did together, he finally managed to take his place in the space-time continuum, emerging from a 'timeless' space (Edwards, 2016). After nearly two years of intensive work, he arrived one day fired up by the opening bars of Beethoven's Fifth Symphony, which his Dad had played at home. He said, 'You wait, then you hear da da da da—then there's a bit of a gap, then da-da-da again—then it starts!' He too had finally 'started' and had taken his place in the space-time continuum, as defined by Einstein, in which physical events are located (three dimensions of space, height, width and depth, linked with one time dimension). He was now able to wait for the sessions and was held as one is held by time, by their regular recurrence.

But as Einstein said in a letter of 21 March 1955 to a bereaved friend (as if to provide some comfort), 'people like us who believe in physics know that the distinction between past, present and future is only a stubbornly persistent illusion'. This view is now orthodoxy among theoretical physicists.

As Schopenhauer said, 'outlandish' ideas, previously ridiculed and resisted, may come eventually to be considered 'self-evident'. These very 'outlandish' ideas, existing in a new land, are gradually adopted by a previously resistant populace. Self-evident indeed … though as with adopted children, there may be an unconscious harking back to the old ways of thinking …

Research findings have indicated that children in long-term foster or adoptive care retain strong feelings for their birth parents and their siblings: these ruptured relationships may remain an internal preoccupation for years, and into adulthood. Margaret Rustin said:

> Adopters usually hope that the 'forever family' will do all that is needed to put right any problems the child may have … once human beings get close to one another, their internal worlds are in a dynamic relation to each other … All the early experiences of each member of any significant relationship contribute to the landscape of the new relationship. Present events can throw into prominence troubling aspects of the past, both providing a chance for a new way forward but also often engendering confusion and distress.
>
> (2023, p. 13)

The development of new relationships in an adoptive family will inevitably be slow and will be plagued by a resurgence of difficulties at points of crisis, as I have indicated. Research undertaken by Dr Miriam Steele at the Anna Freud Centre aimed, by use of the Adult Attachment Interview, to help all those involved in the adoptive process better to assess an appropriate 'fit' between children and adoptive parents. But this is not a one-size-fits-all solution. The central question of the study is one that preoccupies all those involved in this difficult work: 'How can we understand and assess the impact of previous adversities in a child's history on the new relationships that develop between themselves and their adoptive parents?' The interview, which takes the form of an elicited narrative account of parents' own childhoods, was found to be a strong indicator of the attachment status of biological children: secure, avoidant or ambivalent. It was found that it was not so much a difficult history in itself which made for either ongoing entanglement with the story or a defensive dismissal of its relevance, but the way that history had been able to be thought about and digested, so that the adult could look back with some measure of understanding and forgiveness, and make a meaningful assessment of the then and the now. The researchers hope that, by the assessment through stories of particular dilemmas the child might face, they can find out something of the internal world of the child and their view of adults, both before placement and after periods of one and two years after adoption. By linking these findings with those derived from using the Adult Attachment Interview with adoptive parents, which may predict what their assumptions will be about the adoptive child and the prospective relationships they will make together, based on their own early experiences, there can be vital new evidence to help in the placement and ongoing support for the adopted child. But even the most eagle-eyed of us can fail to see the 'surprises' that occur, as I found out when supervising the caseloads of the adoptive team at the Bishop Harvey Family Service. We must forgive ourselves, and move on, learning from the experience.

> We begin at the beginning. But for an adopted child, as I have said, beginnings have been painful, fragmented and often chaotic. With late adopted children, we all become used to hearing the stories of early lives fraught with instability, comings and goings, toings and froings, before events finally become such that the child is 'freed' for adoption. The slow unravelling of emotional ties (or their swift rupture) accompanies the inevitably (and necessarily so) slow external procedures. Inside the mind of the child, there may be huge uncharted areas of confusion and doubt. The 'Life Story Book', which is our adult way of helping the child to make sense of these confusions, may go some way to being a move forward, but may also inevitably leave untouched these uncharted areas of experience. Perhaps this is no bad thing.

It is only during the last 20 years that psychological research has shown that infants and young children are able to recall events in their lives. Freud noted that adults he saw had no recall of early life events and marvelled at 'this remarkable amnesia of childhood ... the forgetting which veils our earliest youth from us and makes us strangers to it'. He thought that early memories were repressed, and that children retained images and fragments of events, but not coherent representations of past experiences. The subsequent observational and clinical experience of child psychotherapists and analysts over the years has put the profession very much in touch with the powerful but unconscious nature of early memories, and it is the verbalisation in the therapy of these that can bring relief. Developmental research has now documented this early capacity to recall events. By demonstrating simple non-verbal sequences to children and infants over progressively longer periods, it has been shown that, as early as 13 months, the capacity to construct and maintain memories of specific events can result in recall over extended periods of time. What was discovered to be crucial was the nature of the events, the number of exposures, and the availability of memory-jogging cues. The researchers talk of 'enabling relations', and by this, they mean events that have coherence. We might, I think, extend this concept to include the enabling relationships which are available, or not, to render events meaningful for the child. For the child who begins life in an environment characterised by its instability, lack of continuity and often its potential for significant harm, where no enabling relationship is available to process events, it is not surprising that there remains an unprocessed swirl of unlinked fragments. This is in stark contrast to the experience for the normal infant and young child within a biological family, whose fears and fantasies are contained, transformed and returned in more manageable form through the reverie of its parents. This vital early experience forms the foundation from which thinking and linking can emerge, and learning and growth can ensue.

How can we, then, think about how to help these troubled and troubling children? I want to quote almost in full a letter written to the *Guardian* newspaper in April 1998, in response to a journalist's piece about government plans for children in care, by the late Andrew Cooper, then Professor of Social Work at the Tavistock Clinic:

> One reason for the breakdown of foster placements (*and, I would suggest, adoptive places too – JE*) is the terrible intensity and complexity of emotional needs arising from the damaging family experiences which children will bring to any substitute care setting. Week by week the qualified social workers I teach bring cases of this kind for discussion; often they feel professionally isolated because they are the only ones prepared to recognise the depth of the child's suffering and disturbance, and the long-term impact of this on prospective carers. The idea of 'small family homes' creates a warm but illusory glow. Staff in such homes will need to be as highly trained and well-supported as anyone in the child care field, if this plan is to do justice to the children involved, and lead to better outcomes.

In this case, one might think of Andrew Cooper as the father, who was able to witness troubles without being destroyed by them. The message is unambiguous: we need across-the-board thinking, training and support, and we need to have an openness to the experience of damaged children, which enables us to enable their carers to meet the demands they make. Being dropped is painful, traumatising and often such a shock as to remain tearless: being picked up gives the child the opportunity to cry. As psychodynamic workers, we have to recognise the need not only to offer help directly to the child but also to be available to consult to their adoptive parents and to the network where these themes may be re-enacted in the adoption process (*and as one of my contributors said, who has dealt with many adoptive children and their placements, 'don't adopt!' – JE*).

As Alison Roy said (2022, pp. 351–361), 'Where possible we should encourage children, adolescents and their adoptive parents to find their own symbols and metaphors.' She herself uses the symbol of nests, drawing on their differences, in the way the poet John Clare, that observer *par excellence*, did many years before her, as did Dostoevsky, in his book, *The Brothers Karamazov*. 'It appears that he changed nests yet a fourth time.' Roy talks of her patients working towards a more authentic version of their life story, and one that brings some relief and healing through the telling. 'They have gone from one nest', as she says, 'or a number of "nests", to one which is strange and new. It may indeed be too overwhelming to hear the whole story, and another kind of splitting may ensue.' I recall (JE) one child carting in his heavy Life Story book to our first session: he was relieved and rather incredulous when I suggested it was life Now that was important. While one child had been referred because of difficulties with his adoptive mother, father too was part of this picture, and it was hard for this boy to attach to either parent. An adopted boy who had been badly abused in his original home, had two contrasting memories that emerged in a therapy session: a flowered stair carpet and a frightening shape at the bottom, which he thought had something to do with hanging coats. (He had, in fact, been found, nearly naked, shut in a cupboard under the stairs.) Whatever the reality on which these images had been based, however, I could simply take it up in terms of fragments (cf. Freud, 1912–1913), good and bad, safe and unsafe, which he was used to carrying around, trying to piece them together. As the aforementioned, Roy (2022) suggests, the 'whole truth' may be just too overwhelming for a young person, already traumatised, to digest. We all have these Proustian images that seem to exist in an area between waking and dreaming, what Rustin (2023) calls 'mental over-crowding' (p. 127), but for the adopted child with no idea of an internal couple who can link together inside his mind and help him think about his story, they can become persecuting and persistent. The non-adopted child in an ordinarily good-enough home with biological parents has to struggle to unite the opposing ideas of loving and hating the same people, biological mother and biological father. The process involves illusion and disillusion on the long road towards an adequate appreciation of reality. For the adopted child, this task may be severely compromised by the facts of early history and the fantasies constructed around them. These internal narratives may remain dormant and then erupt with great force when the child is finally placed for adoption and begins to have a sense of a secure base from which to express a rightful grievance. Are the birth parents bad? Is the child a bad child? Have the adoptive parents stolen the child from an idealised happier situation? This is something I encountered rather frequently in clinical work. It is sobering to note how the most abusive early situations can turn in the child's mind to something loved and lost in the face of the inevitable difficulties of fitting into a new family. As another child said to me, 'I just don't believe they did those things to me.' This was a child who had received substantial 'damages' from the Criminal Injuries Board for the treatment, which had so damaged his beginnings with his birth parents, particularly his father. The often very violent repudiation of knowledge can, as with the myth of Oedipus, re-enter the mind in a similarly violent way, causing further splits because of the difficulty of integrating the facts and the fantasies, in order to achieve a realistic and inevitably mixed picture, both of the birth family and the family of adoption. These conflicts may either persist as a factor inhibiting settling down, or they may re-emerge at times of stress.

References

Bachelard, G. (1969) *The poetics of space*. Beacon Press
Boym, S. (2002). *The future of nostalgia*. Basic Books.
Cusk, R. (2011). Portraits. In *The Guardian review book of short stories*. The Guardian.

Edwards, J. (2016). Towards solid ground. In *Love the wild swan*. Routledge.
Freud, S. (1912–1913). *Totem and taboo*. Hogarth Press.
Jacques, E. (1982). *The form of time*. Crane Russak & Co.
Klein, M. (1963). On the sense of loneliness. In *Envy and gratitude and other works 1946–1963*. Hogarth Press.
Munro, A. (2010). *Too much happiness*. Knopf Doubleday.
Rothstein, M. (November 10, 1986) Canada's Alice Munro finds excitement in short-story form. *New York Times*.
Roy, A. (2022). The challenge of parenting children from different worlds. *Journal of Child Psychotherapy, 48*(3), 351–361.
Rustin, M. (2023). *Finding a way to the child*. Routledge.
Sohn, L. (1983). Nostalgia. *International Journal of Psychoanalysis, 64*(2), 203–211.
Winnicott, D. W. (1971). *Playing and reality*. Tavistock Publications.

10 The Stepfather

In her memoir, *Giving up the Ghost*, Hilary Mantel (2003) talks of the day she moved with her mother, her brothers and Jack, who was first a lodger, then a permanent feature of the household, who would become her stepfather, into a smart new house, fixed up by Jack. Her father was never mentioned again, though she talked to him in her mind. 'Henry, my father, might as well have been dead; except that the dead were more discussed … he was never mentioned after we parted, except by me, to me. We never met again' (p. 153). She is very even-handed in her descriptions; Jack is given a good press, as is her mother. But whose step was it, is it a step up (to the new house), a step down (to the little girl who never sees her birth father again), or a step sideways, from one man to another? In this chapter, we sit on the step, and reflect on how it can lead up or down, or maybe sideways. This is a very different step from Harry's 'naughty step' and is one where we can sit and reflect. We might think too of Charles Dickens's (1850) story of David Copperfield, a boy very close to his single mother, until his stepfather rolled up … Mr Murdstone, what a name indeed, with its combination of 'murderer' and a heart of stone, who made his stepson wear a placard proclaiming, 'this boy bites' … And in 2023, it is not hard to find actual cases where seemingly happy children were then murdered by their envious stepfathers – it is a heartbreaking situation.

Here is an account of a benign stepfather…

> I don't think I am a typical stepfather. I have known Peter (not his real name) since he was born, having visited his mother in hospital as a personal friend very soon after the event. His father left when P was two, and his mother tried to keep his memory sweet enough in Peter's mind. Six years later, I became Peter's stepfather when I moved in to live with him and his mother. His own father, whom I knew, surfaced occasionally. I never tried to take his place and he was talked about openly though (*unlike Mantel's father – JE*), and as I mentioned, he was distant for long periods of time. As Peter and his mother had lived in a communal house, he was used to having many father figures around, and it seemed I was just another one, though rather more present in his life. His mother asked him if he was happy to have me live with them, and

DOI: 10.4324/9781003521846-11

he readily agreed. When my first wife and I separated after a complete breakdown of the marriage, I left behind with some guilty feelings, two children: an adopted girl of 7 and my wife's son of 4 by another relationship. (His own father was absent from his birth, at that time we were still officially married, and so I guess he was also my stepson, though he has always regarded me as his real father.) Peter knew these children, and, as far as I could tell, felt no conflict, though there were initial difficulties because my first wife did not take our separation well, refusing to acknowledge that she had any part in it, and 'blaming' Peter's mother for the split. I don't recall I thought too much about my role in Peter's life, as I had always known him, and there were no difficulties to negotiate as regards my part in his life. I think he took my presence for granted, although the children of my previous relationship found it hard to relate to my current partner for a long time, encouraged by their own mother to reject my second wife's constant friendly overtures. I guess I was a helper and caretaker, and it helped that Peter had known me from birth. I think I always regarded him as a friend as well as a child, for whom I had some responsibility. He is now 45, and there is a close bond between us. I think he valued me being there to support him and his mother, so that as he grew older, he would not have to worry about her so much. I was and still am an important figure in his triangle even though he now has children of his own, who enthusiastically welcome me as 'Grandad'. And, of course, he is an important figure in mine.

References

Dickens, C. (1850). *David Copperfield*. Bradbury & Evans.
Mantel, H. (2003). *Giving up the ghost*. Picador.

11 Rivalry with Fathers

In parent-infant psychotherapy, says Dilys Daws, whose book, *Quietly Subversive*, sums up her superlative approach:

> we may work with two parents and their baby, perhaps an older toddler as well; often we find ourselves seeing just a mother and baby. There are many reasons for this; father is at work, mother needs time to talk by herself, or she says, "he doesn't like talking about the problems." But why are we sometimes secretly relieved to work just with the mother-baby duo? In fact, so much more can happen when fathers are present in the room.
>
> (Daws & Lumley, 2022)

Over 30 years ago, the psychoanalyst David Malan referred a patient of his to Daws for help with her sleepless baby. She met with the family, and in the first meeting, the father who had also been in analysis asked, 'How does the transference work here?' A good question. Daws said, 'I am still working on the answer.' The baby slept through the night after a couple of sessions, but how they got there was complex. These parents were from different countries, different religions, they had both had difficult life experiences, but they were really committed to each other and determined to make life good for their baby. The beginning of each session became a routine. The mother who suffered from post-natal depression would burst into tears, saying she was a bad mother. The father and DD would then, patronisingly, assure her that she was a good mother, doing the best for her baby. After a couple of weeks of this ritual, the mother said, 'Why don't you two go off and get married?' A very timely warning to Daws not to 'capture' either party of the parents and to remain an outsider for them to use as they needed to.

The Oedipus complex is one of the key discoveries of psychoanalysis, the one taken up most enthusiastically into common language, as I have indicated above. Ron Britton (1991) has described how 'the closure of the Oedipal triangle by the recognition of the link joining the parents provides a limiting boundary for the internal world'. He calls this, as we do here, a triangular space. If the link between the parents – perceived in love and hate – can

DOI: 10.4324/9781003521846-12

be tolerated in the child's mind, it allows a third position where the child is a witness not a participant. If he can observe, he can also envisage being observed (see Chapter 9 on seeing and being seen).

Elisabeth Fivaz-Depeursinge has pointed out that when babies interact with one parent while having the other in mind, in parenthesis, their minds will become structured for complex thought (Fivaz-Depeursinge et al., 2009). You could say that differences of opinion, though not hostility, between parents are essential for babies to experience them as separate people. Just like the baby, the therapist may have to tolerate being a witness, not a participant as the family endeavours to understand and repair the ruptures in their relationships.

Are Oedipal conflicts in the family thus mirrored in the therapist? Just as the toddler who climbs into the parent's bed feels that if he literally kicks his father out of it, he will have the perfect union with his mother, do we, male and female therapists alike, feel that we can offer a special relationship to the mother that is interrupted by the father's presence, that he takes away our place? Do we feel that we can manage the mother's views about her baby, but not take on the conflicting views of her partner? We often talk about who is the patient, the mother, the baby, or is it the relationship? This is so much more complex to manage. Taking on the father as well would mean that we ourselves are indeed able to see the world in 3D.

When I hear a passionate story of an enmeshed mother and baby, I think of the mother's relationship to her own mother, of possible unbearable separations, and of the intense ambivalence of love and hate. But I also wonder about the father's role and why the 'intercourse' between the parents is not sufficiently protective to allow the mother and the baby to pull satisfactorily apart. There are often mentions of 'male insensitivity'. Progress may be when the marital issues are eased, and the mother feels able to take the father's advice.

When mothers come with their babies, claiming that father is not interested or does not want to come, it may be felt that she is unfairly representing difficulties in the relationship in a one-sided way. In one instance, I urged the mother to persuade the father to come. To my surprise, he was charming, was attentive to the mother and baby and talked cooperatively with me. After this meeting, the mother never came again. Had I called her bluff – that the father was not as she had described? Or had I been conned, and taken in by false compliance? In either case, perhaps she could no longer trust me.

In a case that Daws and her trainee are currently seeing, the mother comes with the baby. Both are delightful. The mother loves the baby but is unsure of herself in her maternal role and pines for her exciting work life. She envies that father is still able to go out to work and too busy to come to the therapy sessions. I suggested, as I usually do, that she tells him what we talk about when he gets home. She says that she worries that she overloads him already with her doubts about herself and her mothering. She comes to see us in order to spare him. Fathers who do not attend can indeed support the mother's work in the therapy, but this may be mainly at a conscious level. Having the father actually in the room allows him to work at an unconscious level, and, as with the mother, I think working in the presence of the baby is also crucial for the emotional depth of the work.

Bion has described how the mother's thinking about her baby enables him or her to deal with confused emotional experiences in a way that enables the baby to start thinking and dreaming. Daws would add that the mother's dreaming, and also the father's, are part of the process. Parents' dreams may herald progress in dealing with the problems between them and their children. One father dreamed that his little son, Stanley (who could not yet talk), asked him, 'Why don't you show me how to get to sleep?' This released other memories that helped the father connect with similar problems between his own father and himself. The dream linked the past with the present and highlighted that his father's failure to help him as a child was part of the background of his own failure to help his son now. However, Daws thinks perhaps that Stanley's words in the dream – Why don't show me how to get to sleep? – came from a dawning ability in the father to do just that. They show that the father is beginning to imagine himself as being able to help his son. A parent's dreams can be one of the many aspects of caring for their children.

Daws says:

> I have been fortunate to work for a life-time in the NHS in the UK. I think of the State as a kind of father, helping with authority, setting out boundaries. Working with families who are mistreating their children, it is essential to empathise with the difficult experiences that have led to their behaviour, but not to collude with cruel treatment. Without absolving oneself from responsibility, it can be helpful to have this authority in the background. Even with well-functioning families working in the public services, it gives a framework of triangular functioning with the therapy echoing families that include a father.

References

Britton, R., Feldman, M., O'Shaughnessy, E., & Steiner, J. (1991). *The Oedipus complex today*. Routledge.

Daws, D. & Lumley, M. (2022). *Quietly subversive: Selected works of Dilys Daws*. Routledge.

Fivaz-Depeursinge, E., Lopes, F., Python, M., & Favez, N. (2009). Coparenting and toddler's interactive styles in family coalitions. *Family Process, 48*(4), 500–516. https://doi.org/10.1111/j.1545-5300.2009.01298.x

12 Fathers in Poetry

Words come from ways and contexts in which they are used and associations that people make with them, as I emphasised above. Do poems 'open doors', as Robert Frost suggested? How do they read you? Poetry is read, as Neruda said, 'by those who need it', and as Rilke thought, poets are 'bees of the invisible'; they collect the nectar which nourishes our internal world. As the Reverend Ames said to Lila in Marilynne Robinson's novel of the same name, 'Once you start talking, you don't know what you'll say' (Robinson, 2014). This thought excursion begins by taking a line for a walk as Klee suggested; we are helped by opening the door of our academic 'box' to let some light in. As the psychoanalyst Christoph Hering said (personal communication), 'I love to think of poems as texts full with riddles and I avoid any attempt to have the riddles and the confusions and the doubts removed.' The best of psychoanalytic discourse has similar qualities as Bion ([1975] 1990) averred, as well as his dictum that 'psychoanalysis is only one stripe on the coat of the tiger'. I am offering no 'proofs' in this book, but a series of reflections, which hopefully may produce more reflections – what you might call marginal notes perhaps and also some clinical work, done by myself and others. As Anne Alvarez asked in *The Thinking Heart*, 'How do we talk about feelings to children who are cut off from feeling?' (2012, p. 29). Many children growing up without a father may deny that he ever existed. We must always bear in mind the family, social and cultural context.

To quote Graham Music:

> Neglect is about omission not commission, about the effects of not receiving the growth-inducing experiences that help minds grow, emotional lives thrive and hearts come alive. It is being held in mind, understood, thought about, cherished and enjoyed, which gives rise to emotional growth. This is just what neglected children do not get.
>
> (2011, p. 179)

If there is no father in the child's picture, the specific experience of being cherished by a father is lacking, and the opportunity for a particular kind of emotional growth, of being cherished, is lost. What may emerge is a malignant paternal object.

I want to start by talking about a poem many people may know: 'This be the Verse', by Philip Larkin. The very title has a resonant ring, as he says emphatically, take note of this. This poem is of course about both mother and father, and these two figures will be reinstated as internal objects (as psycho-analysts would call them), in each child's mind.

In this relatively short poem, Larkin asserts that your mum and dad 'fuck you up'. He recommends getting out of the parental sphere as soon as you can, as Cat Stevens, the songwriter, also did, and 'don't have any kids yourself'.

If you listen to the link of Larkin reading his poem, you can hear his gloom about man handing on misery to man, and this misery, he thinks, just gets deeper 'like a coastal shelf'. You think the underlying surface is safe, then it suddenly slips away. But people do go on having kids, who develop within the environment of whatever family situation they happen to have been born into. In this chapter the later two poems by Sylvia Plath and Shakespeare will elaborate on this.

Sylvia Plath, whose father died of diabetic complications when she was 8, never found her firm base, as her poem written a few months before her death shows. If you listen to her reading, it is raw indeed: feelings she didn't know she had came bubbling up. (For copyright reasons I am not able to quote the whole poem, 'Daddy', but it is certainly worth listening to it, read by the poet herself, on YouTube: https://www.youtube.com/watch?v=6hHjctqSBwM.) She describes her internal identification with a malignant father, the black shoe in which she lived like a foot, and that she had to resurrect him in order to kill him off in her mind. She is always afraid, she says, but nevertheless fascinated by his cruelty (in her mind), wishing and yet not wishing for 'the boot in the face'. She can see that this malignant identification has persisted, through suicide attempts and a marriage, but in the poem, she feels she is finally taking the phone off the hook, in order to kill his memory off. Nevertheless, one could speculate that she did not achieve this. Feelings bubbled up to overwhelm her. She ends with 'Daddy, I'm through'. What this poem shows us is how without some sort of intervention (therapeutic listening is an excellent way through), the malignancy remains and grows larger inside the mind.

This poem, which can be read as an angry lament against loss, can also be seen as a version of the Electra complex, when the little girl both loves and hates the father who 'deserts' her for mother, or who dies, so she has to resurrect him in order to kill him off again. There is a sado-masochistic tone to this poem that shows the relationship this particular little girl had with her fantasy of the father, which then carried on in her life as an internal object with malignant intent. There is much more that could be said about this poem, but I hope this brief foray into it may set people's own thoughts wandering, and some of them may indeed be painful. Unworked-out feelings about fathers may have lifelong consequences, as is shown in Plath's poem. And they may only surface at a time of crisis, if not thought about previously. As I indicate in my title, insight is at best an 'elusive pursuit', albeit a vital one.

I want to end this book and this thought excursion by quoting Shakespeare's contribution to the canon of fathers. They lie deep within their offsprings' bones, as his poem indicates, and as we find consistently in therapeutic work. In *Wolf Hall*, Mantel puts in the mouth of Thomas Cromwell this memorable idea: 'It's the living that turn and chase the dead. The long bones and skulls are tumbled from their shrouds, and words like stones thrust into their rattling mouths. We edit their writings, we rework their lives' (Mantel, 2009, p. 649). We may change the narrative, and that is our prerogative, but a narrative remains. Or as Shakespeare put it, in *The Tempest*:

> Full fathom five thy father lies;
> Of his bones are coral made,
> Those are pearls that were his eyes,
> Nothing of him that doth fade,
> But doth suffer a sea change
> Into something rich and strange,
> Sea-nymphs hourly ring his knell,
> Ding dong
> Hark! Now I hear them, Ding-dong bell
>   (*The Tempest*, Act 1, Scene 2)

References

Alvarez, A. (2012). *The thinking heart*. Routledge.
Bion, W. R. (1975/1990). *A memoir of the future*. Routledge.
Mantel, H. (2009). *Wolf Hall*. Fourth Estate.
Music, G. (2011). *Nurturing natures: Attachment and children's emotional, sociocultural, and brain development*. Psychology Press.
Robinson, M. (2014). *Lila*. Virago Press.

Conclusion

A film director asked, 'When does a film end?' It's an excellent question, and not just pertaining to film. The images may stay in the mind for a long time after the credits roll. Once our fathers die, they too still remain firmly fixed inside us, as Shakespeare knew – 'nothing of him that doth fade'. What is 'the sea change'? For many people, as my contributors report, memories become sharper and more extensive with age than had been – something strange indeed. As I said in the Introduction, this book concludes that fathers, whether present or absent, and of either sex, are indeed important in the life of every child, in order to be the third point of the Oedipal triangle. In essence, with Bion in mind, the conclusion is to come to your own specific conclusions, to work with specific cases. This book is an invitation to colleagues to carve out their own pathways, forming new associations based on their own experiences and perceptions, carrying on the work that many are already doing. The poems provide a group of images or signifiers that act as poetic shortcuts for certain narratives or trains of thought. Not having had the opportunity to work with the child of same-sex parents, I hope this book may encourage more papers, more thinking about this vital role. For some fathers, the pandemic 'rules' meant home-working and much more input with children, who appreciate having both parents present, where possible (unless this has meant that children have been 'locked up' with abusive fathers, and there has also been a steep rise in mental health referrals). As Fonagy and his colleagues proved, a child may have a different perception of the father compared to the mother: proof indeed that the infant relates in a different way to each parent, and a better relationship with father may mitigate the difficulties experienced both internally and externally with mother. A different reaction is protective and aids the development of reflective-self function, which is the way in which the infant may begin to think about the self. There is, as we might appreciate, something very important about the development of the capacity for emotional reflection and reflective function – that is, the capacity to think rather than act. The experiences that occur within the intersubjective field set up by the attachment relationship will influence the child's sense of self, general development, reactions both to happy and difficult experiences, how she/he sees the world and what happens in terms of the establishment of a repertoire

DOI: 10.4324/9781003521846-14

of defences. As we found in the family service (Edwards & Maltby, 1998), fathers often need to be firmly encouraged to join in the thinking about their referred child, and as Dilys Daws (Daws & Lumley, 2022) says, 'so much can happen when fathers are in the room'.

As Philip Larkin indicated, fathers as well as mothers have an influence, whether benign or malign or a mixture of both, as previous chapters have demonstrated, in the lives of their children. While Larkin's bitter view was of inhumanity deepening 'like a coastal shelf', benign identifications also exist across generations, as I have also indicated here. Intergenerational history, often ignored (see Edwards, Finding the Piggle (2021), is a vital factor in assessment, and one that Winnicott himself apparently did not think about in terms of the case of the Piggle herself. This may be an elusive pursuit, but it is undoubtedly a vital one, and one that becomes clearer as we travel through Fatherland.

Hercule Poirot is a fictional Belgian detective created by British writer Agatha Christie. Poirot is one of Christie's most famous and long-running characters, appearing in 33 novels, two plays, and more than 50 short stories published between 1920 and 1975, so I hope that espousing him in our thinking here, as I did with Miss Marple in *Grandmotherland* (Edwards, 2024) will be a help in sorting out where we are now with Fathers. Hercule, as in Hercules: the Twelve Labours of Hercules, is a myth about the labours that Hercules (Heracles) had to perform as a part of his sentence after killing his own children.

Being one of the offsprings of Zeus' affairs, Hercules has always been the subject of Hera's hatred. It was one of those times of blind hatred that made Hercules lose his mind temporarily, and he killed his own children. After a short while, he was awakened from his state of madness and realized what he had done, with great sorrow and regret. He sought guidance from Apollo and was told by Apollo's oracle that his punishment would be serving his cousin and arch-enemy, Eurystheus, the king of Mycenae and Tiryns for 12 years. For the fifth labour, Eurystheus ordered Hercules to clean up King Augeas' stables. Hercules knew this job would mean getting dirty and smelly, but sometimes, even a hero has to do these things (Yes please, Hercule). Then Eurystheus made Hercules' task even harder: he had to clean up after the cattle of Augeas in a single day.

King Augeas owned more cattle than anyone in Greece. Some say that he was a son of one of the great gods, and others that he was a son of a mortal; whosoever son he was, Augeas was very rich, and he had many herds of cows, bulls, goats, sheep and horses. Hercules said yes, I can clean out all your stables in a single day. Augeas couldn't believe his ears, and Hercules brought Augeas's son along to watch. First, the hero tore a big opening in the wall of the cattle-yard where the stables were. Then he made another opening in the wall on the opposite side of the yard.

Next, he dug wide trenches to two rivers that flowed nearby. He turned the course of the rivers into the yard. The rivers rushed through the stables, flushing them out, and all the mess flowed out the hole in the wall on other side of the yard. Job done. What I hope this book may have done is clear out some of our messy feelings, leaving us with a clearer idea that Fathers (or their equivalent) are important, are vital, that they stand as the third point in the child's triangle of thinking, and their absence is not only regrettable but also, in many cases, catastrophic. As I said at the beginning of this book, it was Stendhal who suggested a book was a mirror walking down a road. What has changed in your particular reflections? Many of us live alongside our histories, enmeshed in them, but unaware. As Larkin asked, 'Where can we live but days?' The 'beautiful mess', which is each one of us, is made up of the everyday stuff of days, largely unnoticed and ignored … to think a little more about this is, I suggest, a version of freedom. As the Roman epigram writer Martial so wisely avers, 'the good person expands the span of his years: to be able to enjoy the life you have spent, live it twice'.

Wroe (2016, p. 84) says of the paintings of Eric Ravilious: 'If all the light by which we see is ancient, having journeyed from the first crack of time, it surely carries with it all manner of memories, disturbances and ghosts.' Perhaps we can have access to such memories and disturbances by and through our thinking, and our memories, here about our fathers, and making links that may sometimes seem uncomfortable, from our first days to our last.

References

Daws, D., & Lumley, G. (2022). *Quietly subversive: Selected works of Dilys Daws*. Routledge.
Edwards, J. (2021). Finding the Piggle: reconsidering D.W. Winnicott's most famous child case. https://doi.org/10.1080/13698036.2021.1996760
Edwards, J. (2024). *Grandmotherland*. Routledge.
Edwards, J., & Maltby, M. (1998). Holding the child in mind: Work with parents and families in a consultation service. *Journal of Child Psychotherapy*, 24(1), 104–133.
Wroe, A. (2016). *Six facets of light*. Jonathan Cape.

Index

absent father 77–100
adolescence 74–75
Adult Attachment Interview 96, 114
Alvarez, A. 97, 100, 112; *Thinking Heart, The* 124
Ames, R. 4
anatomic inferiority 51
Association of Child Psychotherapists 60
'At Home in Renaissance Italy' exhibition (London's Victoria and Albert Museum) 13–15
attachment theory 57

Bachelard, G. 109
Ball, J. 46
Balzac, B.-F. 65–67
Balzac, H. de 65–67
Baptism of Christ, The (National Gallery) 22
Barrows, P.: 'Oedipal issues at 4 and 44' 6–7
Bear, L. L. 8
Berger, J. 59–60; *Ways of Seeing* 58
biological father 1, 36, 82, 91, 117
biological mother 82, 117
Bion, W. 4, 7, 8, 57, 75, 96, 124
Bishop Harvey Family Service 9, 115
Bodichon, B.: 'Reasons for the Enfranchisement of Women' 47
Bohm, D.: *On Creativity* 8
Bowlby, J. 87; attachment theory 57
Boym, S.: *Future of Nostalgia, The* 112–113
'Boys Are Not All Right, The' (Radio 4) 72
Briggs, A. 1
Britton, R. 97, 121–122
Burnett, F. H.: *Secret Garden, The* 62

Calvert, E. 12
Calvino, I. 1

Carroll, L.: *Alice's Adventures in Wonderland* 33
Charmaz, K. 4
Chemaly, S.: *Rage Becomes Her* 60
child development, father's role in 1
Christie, A. 128
Chronicles of Narnia, The 39
Church of England 3
Clare, J. 116
Clinton, B. 82
Cooper, A. 116
Cornwell, D. *see* Le Carré, J.
Critchlow, K. 6
Cromwell, T. 126; *Book of Henry, The* 18–19

daughter's shape, finding 54–63
Da Vinci, L. 13
Daws, D. 123, 128; *Quietly Subversive* 121; *Through the Night* 8
Day, E. 45
Denial 103
despair 61, 62, 98, 110
Diamond, M. J. 35
Dickens, C. 119
Dodgson, C. 33
Dostoevsky, F.: *Brothers Karamazov, The* 116
Doyle, C. 25
Drewitt-Barlow, B. 2–3
Dylan, B. 35, 104

Edwards, J.: *Grandmotherland* 102, 128; *Psychoanalysis and Other Matters* 1
Einstein, A. 35, 113
Emanuel, R. 5, 7
'Event Horizon' exhibition 105–108, 110, 111

'Families Need Fathers' 5
father complex 34–35
father hunger 34, 35
fatherland 102–104
Fenichel, O. 34, 59
Fisher, E.: 'Oh! My Papa' 12
Fivaz-Depeursinge, E. 122
Fonagy, P. 96, 127
Francesca, P. D. 22
Frank, H. 104
Frankenberger, L. 104
Freud, S. 6, 8, 14, 36; *Ego and the Id, The* 21–23; on female development 51; *Future of an Illusion, The* 34; on Oedipus complex 7, 34, 51; on scopophilia 59; on sense of loss 113; structural model of the mind 21; on superego 20, 21; *Totem and Taboo* 34
Friedan, B. 45
Furnish, D. 2

Gardner, C.: *Pursuit of Happyness, The* 72–73
Gatens, M. 46–47
gaze 3–4, 14, 16, 59; male 58
gender dysphoria 51
Goethe, J. W. 23
Gormley, A. 105, 110, 111
grounded theory 4–5
Gurney, J.: *Pieces of Molly: An Ordinary Life* 72, 76

Haggard, L. R. 25, 28, 29
Hare, D. 103
having a father 18–32
Heaney, S. 76; 'Digging' 72
Heing, C. 124
Herman, J. L.: *Father-Daughter Incest* 58
Herzog, J. M. 34; *Father Hunger: Explorations with Adults and Children* 35
Hill, F.: *Memoirs of a Woman of Pleasure, The* 59
Hitler, Adolf 102–104
Hitler, Alois 103
Holocaust 102, 104
Hopkins, J. 19
Horney, K. 51

impersonality of time 113
Infant Observation 15–16
intergenerational haunting 7
Irving, D. 103

Jackson, M. 103
James, C. 36
Jefferies, R.: *Story of My Heart, The* 20
Jobs, S. 82
John, E. 2
Johns, M.: 'The Myth of the One-Parent Family' 95
Joseph, A.: *Sonnets for Albert* 79
Journal of Dad's Death 42–44
Jung, C. 34

Kennedy, R. F. 111
Kids Are All Right, The 2
Klee, P. 8
Klein, M. 23, 57, 70, 75, 109, 113; 'On the Sense of Loneliness' 110
Koppensteiner, R.: *Die Ahnentafel des Führers* ('The Pedigree of the Leader') 104
Kraemer, S.: 'civilisation of fathers, The' 6; 'Origins of Fatherhood, The' 13
Kristeva, J. 51

Larkin, P. 7, 125, 128, 129
Lawrence, D. H. 35
Le Carré, J. 19–20; *Perfect Spy, A* 19
Lion King 72
loneliness 61

Maine, M. D.: *Fathers, Daughters and Food* 35
Malan, D. 121
Mandela, N. 82–83
Mantel, H. 119; *Mirror and the Light, The* 18; *Wolf Hall* 126
Married Woman's Property Act of 1870 47
Married Women's Property Bill of 1868 47
masochism 51
Meier, R. 43–44
mental over-crowding 117
Mill, H. T.: *On Liberty* 45
Mill, J. S. 45–49; *On Liberty* 45; *Subjection of Women, The* 45, 47–49
Milligan, S. 31–32
Milosz, C. 35
Mrs Doubtfire 72
Munro, A. 111
Music, G. 124

narcissism 35, 51
narcissistic personality 75
Nathanson, A. 36
Neumann, E. 34

new fathers 5–8
nostalgia: false 113; reflective 113; restorative 112–113; true 113
Nostalgia 113

Obama, B. 81–82
Oedipus complex 7, 14, 34, 51, 97, 106, 109, 121
omnipotence 87, 96, 109

Pankhurst, E. 47
parent hunger 35
passivity 15, 51
Pick, I. 93
pining 113
Plath, S. 112; 'Daddy' 125
Poe, E. A. 25; *Fall of the House of Usher, The* 53
poetry, fathers in 8–10, 124–126
Presley, L. M.: 'Don't Cry Daddy' 53
progressive disillusionment 6
Pullman, P.: *Northern Lights* 57

Rees, C. 3
Religio Medici 67
Rhode, M.: 'Asperger's Syndrome: A mixed picture' 97; *Invisible Boundaries: Psychosis and Autism in Children and Adolescents* 97; *Many Faces of Asperger's Syndrome, The* 97; *Psychotic States in Children* 97
rivalry with fathers 121–123
Robinson, M. 4, 124
'Role of Father in Psychoanalytic Theory, The' 1
Rovelli, C. 2, 9, 97
Roy, A. 54, 56–57, 60–63, 116, 117; *A for Adoption* 62
Rubik, E. 2
Rustin, M. 114, 117

same-sex parents 2–3, 54–55, 57, 127
Sandler, J. 19
Schicklgruber, M. 104
Schopenhauer, A. 97, 114
scopophilia 59
Segal, H. 7
sense of loss 113
separation-individuation process 108
Shakespeare, W. 9, 126; *Hamlet* 17–18; *Tempest, The* 126
Simpson, O. J. 83
single parent 77–100
Sohn, L. 113
Sprackland, J. 79
Steele, M. 114
stepfather 119–120
Stern, D. N. 57
Stevens, C. 72, 125; 'Father and Son' 7–8
Stockdale-Wolfe, E. 97
Storr, A.: *Human Aggression* 84–85
superego 19–21, 30, 51, 109

unconscious 113, 114
urban warriors 15

Verne, J. 25
voyeurism 59

Waddell, M. 56–57, 63
Wells, H. G. 25
Wheatley, D. 79–80
Wilke, L. D. 62
Winnicott, D. W. 6, 54, 57; 'Hate and the Counter-Transference' 75; on transitional space 108–109
Wollstonecraft, M. 45
Wordsworth, W. 81
Wozniak, S. 82
Wroe, A. 129

Zuppardi, S. 83–84

For Product Safety Concerns and Information please contact our EU
representative GPSR@taylorandfrancis.com
Taylor & Francis Verlag GmbH, Kaufingerstraße 24, 80331 München, Germany

www.ingramcontent.com/pod-product-compliance
Lightning Source LLC
Chambersburg PA
CBHW070938180426
43192CB00039B/2332